SUPERNATURAL

FAITH

in the

New Age

Paul McGuire

Supernatural Faith In The New Age

Paul McGuire

Edited & designed by David L. Young.

DEDICATION

To my darling wife
Kristina McGuire
I love you

ACKNOWLEDGEMENTS

To David L. Young, who had the burning vision to make this manuscript a reality; who tirelessly edited this book; and whose insight and friendship have proved invaluable.

To Bob Whitaker, whose spiritual wisdom and maturity guided this project, along with the important contributions of Joyce Hart and the work of Linda Carson, Cindy Feustel, Valeria Cindric, and Gregg Krissinger at Whitaker House.

Also to my sisters, Frances, Laura, and Caitlin McGuire; my mother Julie, and John; my father William McGuire; Jack and Camie David, who have taught me so much about real love; Denny, Kathy Michael, and Justin.

To my grandmothers, Julie and Grandmere, whose love has made this life easier.

To the true friendship of Franky Schaeffer and Jim Buchfuehrer, who walked the mean streets of Hollywood and New York with me. Thank you, Franky; you are an authentic hero in an age of mediocrity.

To Jeannie Dimter for her wonderful friendship, graciousness, and gourmet cooking and lots of laughter with Nicholas, Lee, and Nitche.

To Rev. Paul and Sharon Moore, Rev. Jim Powers, and Rev. Jack Hayford; the Sunday School and Prayer Room volunteers at the Church On The Way; and Linda Carpenter.

To Wayne Rogers, Michael Christensen, Tim and Cindy McGill, Alana, David Pratt, Mark Weimer, Arthur K. Brian, Bruce, Laura, and Burgess.

CONTENTS

Introduction..9

1. Rise Of The New Age.........................15
2. Who Stole The Rainbow?....................29
3. A Thirst For Truth...........................43
4. The Source Of Power.......................57
5. Highway To Hell............................71
6. The Importance Of Faith..................77
7. Heroes Of The Faith.......................89
8. All You Need Is Love......................103
9. Deliverance From New Age Bondage.....111
10. The Power Of The Spirit.................119
11. Searching For Paradise..................133
12. The Problem Of Reality
    (The Christian Subculture).............147
13. Holy Spirit Dynamite....................155
14. The Curse Is Broken.....................169
15. God's Healing Power.....................179
16. Firewalking & Positive Thinking.......191
17. Commanding The Mountain To Move....205
18. Faith Critics And Robocops............217
19. Who's Evangelizing Whom?.............231
20. Smashing The Gates Of Hell...........241
    Appendix—A Glossary Of New Age Terms.....255
    Notes 259
    Recommended Reading................265
    About The Author...................269

Foreword By
Dick Eastman

One evening actress Shirley MacLaine, the current self-appointed spokesperson for the New Age Movement, was featured on yet another television talk show. Once again she readied herself to spread her views on reincarnation and her supposed past lives in previous generations.

The actress hadn't spoken her second or third sentence when my wife Dee leaned over to me and said, "Honey, please turn that off; it's making me sick."

During prayer the following day, I realized the Lord had been speaking directly to me through my wife's words. I felt God was saying-"I want you to turn off the flow of this false teaching through your prayers. It's making me sick!"

Earlier this year, while speaking at a church near Seattle, Washington, I suddenly felt a dark cloud of spiritual oppression hovering about me. From the pulpit I described the feeling at length and challenged the congregation to begin opposing that oppression immediately through increased praise and spiritual warfare.

After the service, the first person to meet me was a school teacher who asked if I was aware that their church was only a few miles from Shirley MacLaine's new home and only a few miles beyond that was what some consider to be the world headquarters for the New Age Movement itself.

I knew then that my visit to this community was not just a coincidence in my schedule and that God was directing our prayer ministry to mobilize Christians to pray against this satanically inspired teaching. But it wasn't until I read *SUPERNATURAL FAITH IN THE NEW AGE* by Paul McGuire, that I actually got a "handle" on what I was really praying against.

I knew it wouldn't be ordinary prayer that would turn the tide against the New Age. Victory would require *extraordinary prayer* that would capture the full authority of the power of Jesus' name.

I'm especially grateful for Paul McGuire's attempt to bring balance to such controversial themes as "faith teaching" and "prosperity" in light of some of the recent criticisms by a few evangelical authors who think this teaching originated in the "New Age". True, some of this teaching no doubt is excessive, but, as the reader will discover in the following pages, God is still the God of the supernatural and will give His children a supernatural faith to help them effectively engage these satanic forces in victorious warfare.

I get nervous when Christians name names of born-again, Bible teachers and evangelists, calling them propagators of the New Age Movement simply because they speak a positive faith message. I've never been in that "camp" theologically, but I know they love Jesus and are "growing up" in Him just like you and me.

Personally, I believe it is time for believers to stop accusing each other of spreading New Age teaching and instead unite as one to prayerfully cast down the real accuser of the brethren, Satan himself--the true author of the New Age Movement. As believers we need to recognize that one of Satan's chief goals is to keep us so busy judging one another that we're drained of all energy when it comes to the real warfare against the enemy himself.

Although coming from a somewhat differing theological perspective on some issues than the author, I'm convinced *SUPERNATURAL FAITH IN THE NEW AGE* is a book worthy of the widest possible distribution. You, too, may or may not agree with every quote, and you may not hold the author's strong charismatic convictions, but by the last chapter you'll be far better equipped to help pray against the growing influence of the satanically inspired New Age Movement.

DICK EASTMAN, Executive Director
Change the World Ministries
P.O. Box 5838
Mission Hills, CA 91345

Introduction

In recent days, a great deal of criticism concerning what has been termed the "faith movement" and the supernatural dimension of Christianity has come from within the church and without. Faith, positive confession, prosperity, miracles, divine healing, Kingdom theology, the gifts of the Holy Spirit, signs and wonders, and the present day supernatural ministry of Jesus Christ have all come under fire.

We live in a world exploding in crisis, both on the national and individual levels. Divorce, loneliness, disease, business failures, financial problems, psychological ills, drugs and alcohol, sexual chaos, political upheavals, war, crime, pollution, and the threat of nuclear annihilation plague the human race.

Everywhere men and women are crying out, looking for solutions and power to control their lives and world. Technology and the philosophies of secular humanism and scientific materialism have failed to provide lasting answers to the major issues of life. As a consequence, people are opening themselves up to the spiritual realm as never before.

The spiritual war outlined by the Bible between the believers of the personal, living God of the universe and the forces of evil grows with increasing intensity on a daily basis.

On one hand we see a mighty outpouring of God's Spirit as prophesied by the Prophet Joel:

> And it will come about after this that I will pour out My Spirit on all mankind; and your sons and daughters will prophesy, your old men will dream dreams, your young men will see visions. And even on the male and female servants I will pour out My Spirit in those days—Joel 2:28-29.

Millions of people worldwide have personally experienced what first-century Christians experienced in the Upper Room on the day of Pentecost when they were "filled with the Holy Spirit and began to speak with other tongues" (Acts 2:1-4). "Pentecostal" or "charismatic" Christianity is spreading eleven times faster than any other religion in the world.

Concurrent with God's outpouring of the Holy Spirit, however, is a great counterfeit spiritual movement that has been termed the *New Age Movement* (*NAM*). The *NAM* stems from Eastern mysticism and ancient Babylonian religions. It could accurately be termed "Satan's pentecost" because New Age philosophies cause man to worship himself rather than the true God.

Critics of the faith movement and supernatural Christianity accuse major Christian leaders such as Pat Robertson, Dr. Paul Yonggi Cho, Kenneth Copeland, Kenneth Hagin, and others of being influenced by the *NAM* and Eastern mysticism. The idea that Jesus Christ still heals people today and wants to prosper His people is labeled heresy.

It seems as if *faith* itself is on trial—faith in the promises of God's Word, faith in a God who still answers prayer, and faith in the resurrection of Jesus Christ. To make matters worse, recent scandals in the world of Christian television have added fuel to the fire. Terms like "charismatic,"

"fundamentalist," "evangelical," "speaking in tongues,"
"prosperity," and "healing" are now defined at length in
major secular magazines like *Time* and *Newsweek*. Not since
the death and resurrection of the Lord has there been so
much controversy surrounding faith and the message of Jesus
Christ.

Yet despite the dust clouds of confusion and the failings
of some who have espoused "faith" and the gospel of Jesus
Christ, it is vital that we affirm the reality of a God who
cares and still works supernatural miracles in and through
His people. The only reason the *NAM* has become a signifi-
cant force in our world is because it rushed in to fill the
spiritual void left by a church that denied the reality of the
supernatural and turned its back on the teachings of Christ,
who commanded His people to be "clothed with power
from on high" and to "proclaim the gospel of the kingdom."

There is a real danger in labeling the supernatural ministry of Jesus Christ the same as those who teach that, through
faith, miracles are part of the New Age Movement. Signs and
wonders, positive confession, faith teaching, divine healing, prosperity, and the gifts of the Holy Spirit did not
originate from the New Age Movement. They began with
the children of Israel and came to fruition with the church
of Jesus Christ. The *NAM* started to become a world
force when the church began to reject the supernatural
dimension of Christianity.

In this book, we will explore and define what true
Christian faith is and what it isn't. We will expose the false
teachings of the New Age Movement and evaluate some of
those Christian leaders accused of employing its principles
and devices. I pray that readers will approach this matter
with open hearts and prayerfully consider Jesus Christ's
teachings on faith, which is, after all, the foundation of our
life in Him.

A Personal Note

As a word of personal testimony, let me tell you up front that I was deeply involved in Eastern mysticism and the *NAM* for over ten years. I studied and experienced meditation, altered states of consciousness, astral projection, mental telepathy, Buddhism, Hinduism, Zen, the teachings of Baba Ram Dass and Carlos Castaneda, cosmic consciousness, and spirit guides. I rejected "traditional Christianity" because I did not see the kind of power and miracles described in the New Testament experienced in the lives of Christians. Because there was no evidence of the supernatural ministry of Jesus Christ in the churches I came in contact with, I concluded that the gospel of Jesus Christ must be false.

Only after I encountered members of the "Jesus Movement" during the mid-seventies—people who walked and lived in the supernatural power of the Holy Spirit and the realm of the miraculous—was I willing to listen to the message Christians were preaching. When I met people who had the boldness and faith to believe God for miracles, and when I saw "signs" and "wonders" worked among them, then I was convicted by the power of the Holy Spirit.

Until then I had experienced many kinds of supernatural phenomenon, such as "blissful states," "white light," and feelings of tranquility. But when I sensed the presence of the Holy Spirit, something radically different occurred. These people were talking about God and Jesus Christ, and for the first time in my life I felt pure love and a deep sense of truth. All my other mystical experiences seemed artificial in contrast. It was the truth of God's Word set on fire by the Holy Spirit that caused me to reject New Age teachings and accept Jesus Christ as my Lord and Savior.

As a consequence of involvement with the New Age Movement, I fully understand the differences between its teachings and the truth of God's Word. To me, suggestions that the "faith teachers" mentioned previously are influenced by the *NAM* are factually incorrect and even ludicrous. These men teach a Bible-based belief in the supernatural ministry of the Holy Spirit to save, heal, and deliver. This is the essence of authentic New Testament Christianity.

Let's now study this sensitive and timely subject together and try to rescue the baby—faith—from the hands of critics who would throw it out with the dirty bathwater of scandal and unbalanced teaching. Read carefully and thoroughly, expecting the Holy Spirit to "guide you into all the truth" (John 16:13).

CHAPTER ONE

Rise Of The New Age

Standing on the street at Times Square and Broadway, I saw what looked like a wave of darkness roll across the horizon. Giant skyscrapers began disappearing in the distance, and then the lights of entire city blocks flickered and went out. Finally, all around me the glittering and flashing lights of movie marquees and Broadway playhouses vanished. I was in the middle of the great New York City power blackout. Naked terror filled the air as all at once eight million people found themselves alone in the darkness.

Thoughts flashed through my mind: Is this the end of the world? Has a nuclear bomb gone off? I was interrupted by the sounds of splintering glass and screams as looters began plundering the stores that lined the streets. Horrified men and women, many of them tourists, scurried out of Broadway theaters. Holding hands, many people formed long lines in an attempt to protect themselves and find their way home.

I felt as though civilization had instantly disappeared and all that remained was an endless jungle of concrete and steel. It was a perfect illustration of science and technology's failure to provide the answers to people's spiritual needs. As a result, men and women feel powerless to meet the challenges of life.

In his book, *Future Shock*, Alvin Toffler writes,

> Today mounting evidence that society is out of control breeds disillusionment with science. In consequence, we witness a garish revival of mysticism. Suddenly, astrology is the rage. Zen, yoga, seances and witchcraft become popular pastimes. . . . We are told it is more important to feel than to think as though there were a contradiction in the two. Existential oracles join Catholic mystics, Jungian mysticism of the East which claims to offer direct experience rather than dead ritualism.[1]

People feel powerless to deal with basic issues such as money, relationships, health, opportunities, peace, sex, God, death, and other things that seem beyond their control. This is the reason for the spread of New Age philosophy. It promises to provide answers, restore order, and give an individual the power to handle life.

Nothing is wrong with desiring the power to control the forces in your environment or wanting the wisdom to understand the deeper issues of life. This desire has been placed within us by our Creator. The question is, "How does one go about doing it?" What many Christians do not understand—especially those who criticize the faith movement—is that God wants His people to rule in the affairs of life and have dominion over their circumstances.

The New Age Counterfeit

Actress Shirley MacLaine has popularized a distillation of Eastern mystical and occult practices that have come to be called the *New Age Movement*. Her book and television movie, *Out On A Limb*, have influenced thousands.

The *NAM* is a diverse group of individuals and groups who hold a common belief that man *is* "God" when he discovers or "awakens to" who he or she really is through a process of "enlightenment." The *NAM* has been gathering increasing strength over the last several years. New Agers across the planet recently gathered together in places like Central Park in New York City and the great pyramids in Egypt to celebrate a day of "Harmonic Convergence." During this celebration, participants "hummed" in unison in an effort to raise the consciousness of the planet and accomplish their goal of bringing about the dawning of the New Age and a one-world government.

Essentially, the *NAM* is a satanic counterfeit of New Testament Christianity. It is a false gospel of salvation that denies the truth of God's Word and the Lordship of Jesus Christ. As such, it is a religious movement spawned in hell, not in heaven.

This does not mean that many New Agers aren't sincere in their desire for peace and love to reign supreme on earth. For many people, Christianity challenges their fundamental view of reality and the universe. Even as I write these words in the hills above Hollywood, people like Timothy Leary, the Harvard psychologist turned LSD prophet, live just up the street from me. As I consider the ashrams and meditation centers tucked in the mountains all around, I realize that for this geographic location, which has an amazing influence on the rest of the world, the Judeo-Christian world view is in the minority.

Truth, however, is not and never was determined by popular vote. There was a time when the majority of the world's population thought the earth was flat, but that did not make it true. When Noah built the Ark, the people living around him laughed—until the rains fell. Truth is never determined by consensus but by fact.

Many people feel severely alienated when they hear about Christianity. They think about the PTL Club and any number of things. As I was growing up in New York City, I literally hated Christians and the church. In fact, when I used to walk to the subway on Sunday morning to go to Central Park and participate in the "Be-Ins" and "Love-Ins" of the sixties, I would pass by churches and spit on their sidewalks.

My hatred of Christianity grew so intense during college that I planned to steal the large gold crucifixes out of the church as an act of defiance. As a radical activist, I believed that Christianity was the "opiate of the people." I thought that Christians, with their barbaric religion, would prevent the "revolution" and a "higher consciousness" from coming to our world. Sharing Erich Fromm's point of view in *The Art of Loving,* I felt that Christianity and the belief in God was a primitive level of social development that should be transcended.

Like many involved in the *NAM*, I was seduced and brainwashed to believe that there are many ways to heaven and that there is no such thing as evil incarnate or a devil. In this incorrect view of reality, I falsely believed that all evil could be attributed to ignorance or psychological problems. Basically, I subscribed to the belief that man is basically good and in the process of evolving into a higher realm of consciousness or development. Secular humanists and people who embrace Eastern mystical philosophy share a common belief in evolution either from the biological perspective of Charles Darwin or in the Hinduistic sense of reincarnation. Both ideas are based on the deception that man is moving into a higher state of being.

Cosmic Consciousness
Or Dangerous Deception?

My involvement in the *NAM* led me to practice techniques such as higher consciousness, mental telepathy, astral projection, meditation, etc. I can say unequivocally that it was *not* the emphasis on the supernatural and miracles stressed by ministers like Pat Robertson and Kenneth Hagin that drew me toward the New Age. I rejected the claims of Jesus Christ because I did not see any evidence of the Holy Spirit in the church. Had I encountered Christians who moved in the power of the Holy Spirit or emphasized biblical "faith" earlier in my life, I would have accepted Jesus Christ as Lord and Savior. Basically, I was looking for proof that He was who He claimed to be.

The supernatural phenomenon I experienced allowed me to enter a higher realm of consciousness, where "spirit beings" communicated with me and I exercised psychic powers. I learned to cause certain events to happen in my life, and I could control people with my thoughts. Attaining what is termed "cosmic consciousness," I saw "white light" and regularly traveled to higher realms of consciousness on the "astral plane."

As a result of these experiences, I had serious doubts when I encountered "Bible-believing" Christians who told me that Jesus Christ was "the only way to God." I could agree that Jesus Christ was an "enlightened teacher," but I found it difficult to accept that He was the Son of God. I asked myself, If Jesus Christ rose from the dead and performed the miracles outlined in the Bible, and if the New Testament Christians were filled with a wondrous love and power that turned the world upside down, then why are all the churches I visit so dead and lifeless?

Unlike many Christians, I didn't have any theological problems about miracles or the supernatural. As a New Age practitioner, the supernatural was already a part of my daily life. I kept asking myself, If Jesus Christ is "the Way, the Truth, and the Life" then why don't I see any evidence in the lives of Christians? I deduced that Christianity must be a primitive religion adhered to by people who exist on a lower plane of consciousness. Unfortunately, I didn't see any evidence to the contrary.

As a consequence, I deepened my *NAM* activities, believing the lie that I was working out my "karma." Soon, I thought, I would free myself from the "wheel of births and deaths" and achieve enlightenment. If I could become an enlightened being, I thought, then I would no longer have to reincarnate to this planet. I would achieve "Godhood."

Facing The Truth

After many years of research and Bible study, however, I have to state emphatically that God's Word has been right all the time in declaring that man is sinful and in need of a Savior. There is a devil and demons, and the only way to heaven is through faith in Jesus Christ. In a nutshell, it is important to understand that *there is absolute truth in the universe, and a belief that is not true is false and therefore a lie.*

This is a big pill to swallow for those who have embraced the "Village Voice-L.A. Weekly-Frank Zappa-MTV-I'm okay-you're okay" mind-set. Millions of people in our world today are in the grip of a false view of reality. They are discovering that a new Mercedes Benz, a *Playboy Magazine*, sexual fantasy, cocaine, meditation, and an American Express Gold Card don't satisfy the deepest longings in the human heart.

Vast segments of our society do not acknowledge the full reality of the death, resurrection, and Lordship of Jesus Christ. They buy into the world system promoting the idea that happiness comes from climbing the corporate ladder or becoming a rock 'n' roll or movie star. The generation of "flower children" who mocked their parents' materialism has become one of the most materialistic generations ever. Counseling centers are flooded with the members of this lost generation, who suffer from depression and anxiety in increasing numbers. Psychologists tell us that people are obsessed with brand labels, designer jeans, fancy automobiles, and the right address because they are insecure and do not love themselves.

Despite this "fall out" from the sixties and mid-seventies, our society continues to move down the path of humanism and mysticism. Many in the educational system, mass media, creative community, political arena, medical establishment, and business world do not believe in the Judeo-Christian God. The apostle Paul had this to say about the situation: "For the word of the cross is to those who are perishing foolishness, but to us who are being saved it is the power of God" (1 Corinthians 1:18).

Who Is God?

Today's society exhibits both hostility to the message of Jesus Christ and an unprecedented openness among people who are hungry to hear the gospel. I entered a health food store in Coldwater Canyon here in Los Angeles and browsed through the magazine rack. The majority of the magazines on diet and nutrition had strong New Age leanings, with articles on meditation, higher consciousness, guru's, etc. One article attacked "evangelical," "fundamentalist," and "charismatic" Christians while it applauded

Eastern mystical philosophies. In his epistle to the Romans, the apostle Paul warned against unbelief and its consequences:

> For the wrath of God is revealed from heaven against all ungodliness and unrighteousness of men, who suppress the truth in unrighteousness, because that which is known about God is evident within them; for God made it evident to them. For since the creation of the world his invisible attributes, His eternal power and divine nature, have been clearly seen, being understood through what has been made, so that they are without excuse.
>
> For even though they knew God, they did not honor Him as God, or give thanks; but they became futile in their speculations, and their foolish heart was darkened. Professing to be wise, they became fools, and exchanged the glory of the incorruptible God for an image in the form of corruptible man and of birds and four-footed animals and crawling creatures. Therefore God gave them over in the lusts of their hearts to impurity, that their bodies might be dishonored among them. For they exchanged the truth of God for a lie, and worshipped and served the creature rather than the Creator, who is blessed forever. Amen—Romans 1:18-25.

The bottom line with the New Age Movement is that they exchange the "truth of God for a lie" and worship and serve "the creature rather than the Creator." The *NAM*, as well as many other false religions, teaches that man is God and that he must "awaken" to this fact.

Stewart Brand, founder of the *Whole Earth Catalogue*, once commented that "man is God and we better get good at it." Since we are "gods," he reasoned, we should learn to behave and act like it so we can run the universe. This is the same lie that the serpent used to seduce Eve in the Garden of Eden when he said, "You will be like God, knowing good and evil" (Genesis 3:5).

Man is a powerful being made in the image of God, and he has many god-like qualities. Ultimately, however, we must understand that man is *not* God. Each of us must take our proper position before the Lord, bow our hearts, and worship Him. For indeed, He alone is King of kings and Lord of lords.

The current trend toward *NAM* philosophy is not neutral. The business community, government, schools, military, and organizations like Alcoholics Anonymous have been inundated with a flood of New Age teaching disguised as "relaxation techniques," "stress management," "creative problem solving," and "healing your inner child."

The question we must raise is, "Do these practices move people closer to their Creator, or do they establish a rebellion from God?" Which direction do these activities take people in? Do they move them toward recognizing that they are separated from God and in need of the saving grace of Jesus Christ? Or do they teach that men and women must look deep within themselves and "discover that they are 'God' "? Obviously, both of these world views cannot be correct simultaneously. One must be correct and the other false. Anything that instills the belief that man is the center of the universe is wrong.

The clash between these world views goes back to the story of Cain and Abel. Genesis 4:2 tells us that Abel was "a keeper of flocks," or a shepherd, and Cain was "a tiller of the ground," or a farmer.

In the course of time, both Cain and Abel brought an offering to the Lord. It must be remembered that, as the direct descendants of Adam and Eve, they had parents who knew God intimately. Despite the Fall, Adam and his wife passed this knowledge on to their children. Therefore, Cain and Abel knew what was acceptable to God and what was not.

Cain brought an offering of fruit to the Lord—something that he grew himself out of the ground. It was an offering based on self-effort. Abel gave God a different kind of offering. He brought the "firstlings of his flock" as a sacrifice to the Lord. At the very beginning of history, therefore, we see mankind approaching God from two diametrically opposed viewpoints—one through self-effort, or "works," and the other through the blood of a sacrificed lamb. Thousands of years later, God sacrificed His first-born Son—the "Lamb of God"—on a blood-stained cross to save the human race from sin.

The *NAM* teaches that we should approach God through self-effort, "working out our own karma," or the "fruit of our own spiritual labor." This is the way of Cain, and it does not please God. It is interesting to note that part of the Transcendental Meditation (*TM*) ceremony and other Hindu ceremonies involves offering fruit to the guru. This is the same mistake Cain made. Eventually, he murdered his brother because of jealousy.

What is Reality?

We must understand that Jesus Christ is not just another way to heaven. Biblical Christianity and *NAM* philosophy take us in entirely different directions. To understand fully the conflict between Christianity and New Age teaching, we must understand the true nature and composition of reality.

The Word of God teaches about a parallel reality to the one we are living in and that all of life has a spiritual dimension. Scripture goes on to describe a war being raged on Planet Earth for the hearts and minds of men between Jesus Christ—the Lord of the universe—and a powerful spiritual being named Lucifer, or Satan. This evil ruler, who has organized a rebellion against God, has many forces, including one-third of all the angels.

> And there was a war in heaven, Michael and his angels waging war with the dragon. And the dragon and his angels waged war . . .
>
> And the great dragon was thrown down, the serpent of old who is called the devil and Satan, who deceives the whole world; he was thrown down to earth, and his angels were thrown down with him—Revelation 12:7, 9.

My fervent prayer is that the truth of God's Word shatters any misconceptions you might have concerning the multi-dimensional nature of reality and the war being waged between heaven and hell. This is contrary to everything taught in *NAM* philosophy, which does not acknowledge the battle between God and the devil. But this is the exact reason why Eastern mysticism and New Age thought is deception. If, indeed, there is a battle between God and the devil involving all of mankind, then it would be total deception to teach that there isn't.

I realize that this is heavy stuff for people indoctrinated into a philosophy that does not acknowledge good and evil. In New Age and mystical philosophy, only duality, or positive and negative *yin* and *yang* (which are both parts of the "cosmic whole"), is taught.

In other words, the New Ager does not believe in the concept of evil but *illusion*. An atrocity like the murder of millions of Jews during the hideous reign of Adolph Hitler is considered "maya" or illusion and the burning away of "karma." *NAM* teachers suggest that somehow the Jews brought this on themselves or attracted it on a spiritual plane.

Mind Control

New Age teaching is not only harmful but very dangerous because it desensitizes the soul and conscience of man in relation to the horrors of evil and sin. Nazi Germany, the present day holocausts carried out by communists and terrorists across the globe, abortion, and violent crime are *not* "illusion." They are acts of evil with painful consequences.

This is why New Age teaching is not just a spiritual pursuit but a satanically inspired program of deception that systematically desensitizes men and women and lays the groundwork for total domination by evil. Every *NAM* and Eastern mystical teaching trains people toward passivity. Meditation, "mantras," "chants," and "humming" empty the conscious, rational mind so a person can come in contact with the "divine spirit within."

Passivity of the mind and "going with the flow" prepares people for domination by either a guru or a totalitarian government. Passive people with no clear concept of good and evil do not possess the inner moral and spiritual strength to resist evil either in the form of a strong spiritual leader or a dictator. This is why we hear about so many accounts of control, domination, and abuses by gurus and *NAM* teachers like Werner Erhard of EST, Bhagwan Shree Rajneesh, etc.

Within the context of many New Age disciplines, people submit themselves to rigid forms of personal restriction and discipline. Large sums of money are paid to spiritual leaders, and there seems to be an increased willingness to subjugate everything. This is a form of spiritual totalitarianism or dictatorship, and it is rampant in the *NAM* because of the pervasive teaching that encourages passivity of the mind and relinquishing control over to a single authoritarian leader.

Stripped to its bare essentials, New Age teaching is subtly preparing its followers to pledge allegiance to the antichrist. Spiritual leaders are deliberately moving their followers away from the Lord Jesus Christ and setting the stage for the worship of this satanically inspired world dictator.

Again, I understand these words are strong medicine for people who say nothing is wrong with practices like meditation or a belief in reincarnation. In understanding the New Age Movement, however, we must understand the force behind it. To do that we must have a clear understanding of what the Bible says about spiritual conflict.

(For more detailed definitions of New Age terminology, see the Appendix.)

CHAPTER TWO

Who Stole The Rainbow?

After sending the Genesis flood, God gave us the rainbow as a promise that He would never again destroy the earth in such a manner. The rainbow does not belong to the New Age Movement but to God and His people.

Just as the New Age Movement as a whole is a counterfeit of biblical Christianity, many *NAM* practices are satanic copies of the work of the Holy Spirit. In fact, certain cable television shows offer a kind of demonic imitation of Christian television.

The Satanic "Pentecost"

Let's consider *channeling*, which is popular in Los Angeles. Movie stars and housewives flock to channelers. Basically, the person involved in channeling opens himself or herself up to a spirit-being, who uses the channeler's mouth and body to communicate various messages. This spirit-being usually has a name and a different tone of voice and can give people a supernatural understanding of events occurring in their lives. I saw a video tape of Shirley MacLaine sitting at the feet of one channeler, apparently mesmerized by every word.

Since my wife and I are both involved in the film industry, I as a producer and she as an actress, we are in continual contact with actors and other people who work with motion pictures. Many of them are deeply involved in the *NAM*. In fact, while MacLaine was doing the post-production work on her film, *Out On A Limb*, she used the same facility that Franky Schaeffer and I used when working on a feature film. One of the engineers told us that MacLaine would often go into a private room to consult a spirit-guide concerning editing decisions.

All of this is a counterfeit of biblical Christianity. It is a satanic "pentecost" with an outpouring of deceiving, seducing evil spirits. The practice of channeling is counterfeit to being baptized in the Holy Spirit. Instead of getting filled with the Holy Spirit, however, channelers are opening themselves up to unholy, demonic entities. It is this entity that begins to speak through them.

As these spirit-beings speak, they often mimic the supernatural gifts of the Holy Spirit called the "word of wisdom," the "word of knowledge," "gifts of healing," and "the effecting of miracles." (See 1 Corinthians 12.) While Christians debate whether or not these gifts are for today, the devil uses all sorts of supernatural "gifts" to draw people to himself—unfortunately, he is succeeding.

In the twelfth chapter of First Corinthians, the apostle Paul talks about the gifts of the Holy Spirit:

> Now concerning spiritual gifts, brethren, I do not want you to be unaware . . .
> Now there are varieties of gifts, but the same Spirit. And there are varieties of ministries, and the same Lord. And there are varieties of effects, but the same God who works all things in all persons. But to each one is given the manifestation of the Spirit for the common good. For to one is given the word of wisdom through the Spirit, and

to another the word of knowledge according to
the same Spirit; to another faith by the same Spirit,
and to another gifts of healing by the one Spirit,
and to another the effecting of miracles, and to
another prophecy, and to another the distinguish-
ing of spirits, to another various kinds of tongues,
and to another the interpretation of tongues. But
one and the same Spirit works all of these things,
distributing to each one individually just as He
wills—1 Corinthians 12:1-11.

The Mask Of The Deceiver

Obviously, the Lord intended His church to use and
operate in the supernatural gifts of the Holy Spirit. Otherwise, He wouldn't have given such detailed instructions
about them in the Bible. Some Christians insist that the gifts
of the Holy Spirit ended with the apostles. Meanwhile, the
prince of darkness, Satan, is having a field day giving the
people he uses all sorts of supernatural gifts to draw others
into evil.

"Then if any one says to you, 'Behold, here is
the Christ,' or 'There He is,' do not believe him.
For false Christs and false prophets will arise
and will show great signs and wonders, so as to
mislead, if possible, even the elect. Behold, I have
told you in advance"—Matthew 24:23-24.

Numerous passages in the Bible warn about the deceiving activity of the evil one. The devil is a liar and a deceiver,
and his number-one strategy is convincing people he doesn't
exist. It is under the camouflage of his supposed non-
existence that Satan can accomplish all kinds of things.

The mockery in our culture of a belief in an intelligent, personal devil is very dangerous, for it disarms people to the brutal reality of evil. The idea of the devil running around in a red suit with horns, a tail, and a pitchfork is part of the humor the enemy uses to hide his evil handiwork. People who do not understand the nature and reality of the spiritual warfare occurring on our planet are ripe for deception because they falsely assume that all miracles are from God.

> . . . that is, the one whose coming is in accord with the activity of Satan, with all power and signs and false wonders, and with all deception of wickedness for those who perish, because they did not receive the love of the truth so as to be saved. And for this reason God will send upon them a deluding influence so that they might believe what is false—2 Thessalonians 2:9-11.

Channeling, miracles from gurus, and supernatural experiences outside from the Word of God are satanic— period. Any supernatural act performed by a person who does not acknowledge Jesus Christ as God and that the only way to be saved is through faith in Christ is a counterfeit, and the person is a deceiver. They are performing false wonders, and a deluding influence is upon them. Revelation chapter thirteen talks about the beast who was allowed to deceive people from the truth.

> And he performs great signs, so that he even makes fire come down out of heaven to the earth in the presence of men. And he deceives those who dwell on the earth because of the signs which it was given him to perform—Revelation 13:13-14.

The key thing to understand here is that *there is* an evil spiritual being who deliberately and systematically deceives people. The New Age Movement is not all flowers, peace, and "good vibrations." The dark unseen force behind it all is using and manipulating people for evil purposes. If you could rip the mask off the front of a smiling guru, you would see a hideous demon.

Biography Of The Devil

C.S. Lewis said, "There are two equal and opposite errors into which our race can fall into about devils. One is to disbelieve in their existence. The other is to believe and feel an excessive and unhealthy interest in them."[1]

Our culture holds both of these errors simultaneously. On one hand, authors like Stephen King (*Carrie, The Shining,* etc.) and William Peter Blatty (*The Exorcist*) make fortunes writing about evil, and moviegoers flock to the theatres to watch the latest horror film. On the other hand, people laugh at the idea and concept of Satan.

The Bible talks at length about a spiritual battle between Satan and God. Satan, originally called Lucifer, was once one of the highest angels in the angelic realm. He enjoyed the unique privileges of unequaled beauty, intelligence, power, and authority. In times past, Lucifer was a good angel who lived perfectly before God. The Old Testament prophet Ezekiel talks about the life of an ancient ruler called the King of Tyre. In reality, the King of Tyre was Satan.

> "You had the seal of perfection, full of wisdom and perfect in beauty. You were in Eden, the garden of God; every precious stone was your covering: the ruby, the topaz, and the diamond; the beryl, the onyx, and the jasper; the lapis lazuli,

the turquoise, and the emerald; and the gold, the workmanship of your settings and sockets, was in you. On the day you were created they were prepared.

"You were the anointed cherub who covers, and I placed you there. You were on the holy mountain of God; you walked in the midst of the stones of fire.

"You were blameless in your ways from the day you were created, until unrighteousness was found in you"—Ezekiel 28:12-15.

Lucifer was dazzlingly beautiful and held an exalted position as the leader of the angels—until unrighteousness was found in him. What was this unrighteousness that was found in Lucifer? The prophet Isaiah explains:

How art thou fallen from heaven, O Lucifer, son of the morning! how art thou cut down to the ground, which didst weaken the nations! For thou hast said in thine heart, I will ascend into heaven, I will exalt my throne above the stars of God: I will sit also upon the mount of the congregation, in the sides of the north: I will ascend above the heights of the clouds; I will be like the most High—Isaiah 14:12-14 *KJV.*

The unrighteousness found in Lucifer was that *he wanted to be God.* He wanted to sit on the throne of God and rule the universe. This is the lie of humanism and the *NAM.* They seduce men and women by telling them they are God. New Age philosophy teaches people to look deep within themselves and discover "God-consciousness," or "higher consciousness,'' which is another way of stating that you are to awaken to the fact that you and God are the same.

When Lucifer revolted against God, one-third of the angels in heaven followed him.

> And the great dragon was thrown down, the serpent of old who is called the devil and Satan, who deceives the whole world; he was thrown down to the earth, and his angels were thrown down with him. . . .
> And his tail swept away a third of the stars of heaven, and threw them to the earth—Revelation 12:9, 4.

Demons are fallen angels in rebellion from God who have decided to follow Satan. Lucifer is *Satan*, which means "adversary," or *the devil,* which means "accuser." He hates mankind as God's crowning creation.

All the great evils in history can be attributed to the work of Satan on this planet. Evil is not an accident or the result of complex psychological factors. Satan is an evil, twisted, and warped spiritual being. He has an absolute hatred for the things of God and is in open rebellion against God's Kingdom. The devil's objective is to enslave and destroy mankind. Mass murderers like Charlie Manson and Adolph Hitler, cults, wars, violence, torture, and sexual perversion are all evidence of the powers of darkness at work in our world.

The greatest war in the history of the universe was not World War I, World War II, or even World War III should it ever come. The greatest war in all the universe is going on right here on planet earth, and most people don't even realize it! They have been lulled to sleep and hypnotized by the world system. The movie, *Night Of The Living Dead*, about the zombies who walk the earth, is not as far-fetched as one might think. Lucifer has hypnotized the human race into believing that this life is all there is.

Blinded By The Light

You can blind a person by shining a bright light in their eyes. It is no accident that Lucifer means "the shining one" and that "the god of this age" is Satan. He has blinded many people with the dazzling false "white light" of deception.

> And even if our gospel is veiled, it is veiled to those who are perishing, in whose case the god of this world has blinded the minds of the unbelieving, that they might not see the light of the gospel of the glory of Christ, who is the image of God—2 Corinthians 4:3-4.

This is why so many people cannot see or hear the truth of Jesus Christ. It's as if they were living in a kind of trance. If, indeed, as the Bible declares, Jesus Christ died on a cross and was raised from the dead for the sins of mankind—and if He is the Son of the living God—then to ignore this greatest fact of history and turn your back on Him is absolute madness.

Yet this is exactly what multitudes of people are doing. Millions of men and women are living their lives out and pretending there is no God, no devil, and no eternal death. By suppressing the reality of God, death, and judgment, they are living in a deluded fantasy world. The god of this world has blinded them.

An Angel Of Light

If the devil can't get someone to reject their beliefs, he will try and steal their faith in God through other means of deception. Lucifer's favorite disguise is to come as an "angel of light":

> For such men are false apostles, deceitful workers, disguising themselves as apostles of Christ. And no wonder, for even Satan disguises himself as an angel of light—2 Corinthians 11:13-14.

I had to learn this the hard way.

After being a Christian for a year, I still had difficulty believing that the devil was real. Having been indoctrinated with the idea that all evil was due to ignorance or psychological problems, I couldn't come to terms with the reality of evil personified. In fact, even though I believed in Jesus Christ as the Son of God, I still thought there could possibly be more than one way to God. After all, I thought, didn't Gandhi, Buddha, and Mohammed have equally valid things to say?

One afternoon while I was doing some volunteer work for a Christian ministry called the Manhattan Project, a young man came into the office. He said, "Hi, my name is Jim. I'm from the Divine Light Mission and the Guru Mahara Ji." He began to talk about all the good things his guru was doing. "We have ecological programs to improve our environment, and we are trying to build a wholesome spiritual community. We encourage and teach the principles of love, peace, and brotherhood."

I was fascinated by what he was saying and said to myself, How can any Christian say that what he is talking about is evil or accuse his guru of being satanic? Jim was talking about everything I believed in—love, peace, brotherhood, and ecology.

My many years in mysticism, however, made me aware that, as Jim was talking to me, he was silently chanting a mantra and focusing spiritual energy at me. Sensing vibrations coming at me from where he was sitting, I felt a supernatural force enter the room. It was *not* like the presence of the Holy Spirit.

As this sensation grew stronger, a very confusing, intense spirit began bombarding me. I became almost overwhelmed by this supernatural energy, when, all of a sudden, I stood up and rather loudly asked Jim to leave. My head was spinning. Reaching for the phone, I called several Christian friends. They pleaded the blood of Jesus Christ upon me and bound the spirit of confusion and the occult force that was in the room. Soon my confusion gave way to the joy and peace of the Holy Spirit.

I have never forgotten the painful lesson I learned that day: Just because someone talks about love, joy, peace, harmony, ecology, and brotherhood does not mean they are from God. Beware of the angel of light, for after he blinds, he devours.

The Master Of Seduction

The only reason the New Age Movement even exists is because it promises to meet the needs of hurting people. Shirley MacLaine said in one of her *Los Angeles Times* articles,

> Dare we understand that we can make a difference? Dare we believe that we have access to wise and divine spiritual knowledge?

> New Age consciousness doesn't believe these
> things. It knows them. And that knowledge is
> setting people free . . . from fear, rage, anxiety,
> anger, frustration, helplessness, futility and will-
> ful destruction.[2]

In all his deceptive brilliance, Lucifer knows where the
"hot buttons" of mankind are. While Christians argue about
theology and play religious games, the father of lies subtly
lays a trap for the human race by promising to meet the needs
of people that Jesus Christ already died for. The devil is a
counterfeiter, and the only reason he is getting away with
this diabolical plot is because Christians are not preaching
the gospel of the Kingdom. Faith teaching is not to blame—it
is the solution!

The crafty, subtle "serpent of old" is a master of cunning
and seduction. But the only way he can seduce mankind
is to get people to doubt God's integrity and goodness.
Slithering around on his belly, Satan tries to convince men
and women that Christianity is a religion of death and
archaic concepts. When I was involved with the *NAM*, I
believed the devil's lie. This is precisely what millions of
spiritually hungry people believe today. Christianity is not
even an option for them because they have been deceived
into believing it is a lifeless, ugly religion that will not meet
their needs.

Christians who do not understand the power of God's
Word fall right into Satan's game plan because they short-
circuit the miraculous power of God with doubt and
unbelief. As a result, people embrace the New Age Movement instead. Can you blame them? The *NAM* offers
healing for their bodies and minds, the unleashing of
human potential, full creative expression, and the power to
control adverse circumstances. It is filled with thinking,

articulate, and animated people: actors, actresses, film producers, rock 'n' roll stars, successful businessmen—the movers and shakers of society.

Don't kid yourself—the devil knows how to sell and package his product. New Age books and magazines, rock 'n' roll album covers, pornography, drugs, cigarette advertisements, and liquor displays all falsely promise life and excitement.

But it is all lies and seduction! The answer for mankind—for healing and the release of human potential—is the gospel of Jesus Christ. Aside from several notable exceptions, however—and most specifically the faith teachers—we have not been preaching this truth. Today's culture has a distorted imitation of Christianity; it is not the real thing. How do we know it is not the real thing? Because it does not conform to what the Bible says about Christianity. The Book of Acts clearly states what happens when real Christianity is being practiced: "And everyone kept feeling a sense of awe; and many wonders and signs were taking place through the apostles" (Acts 2:43).

Focusing On The Gospel

The following analogy will explain the current problem in Christianity and offer a solution.

We are in the middle of a video-cassette revolution that has transformed the entertainment industry. People who own home videocassette recorders can make copies of any videotape through a process known as *duplication*. In duplicating a tape, one starts with the original or "master tape" and makes a copy onto another machine. The copy is never as clear as the original because it is, in video terminology, a "generation" away from the master tape.

If you were to make a copy of the copy, you would have an even more distorted version because you would now be two generations from the original. If you continued this process of copying your copies, eventually you would become so many generations away from the original master tape that the product would be practically unwatchable. The picture would be too fuzzy and distorted.

A similar thing has taken place with the preaching of the gospel. When Jesus Christ originally preached the gospel of the Kingdom to His disciples, it was only one generation away. In other words, Jesus Christ was the original, and the apostles and first-century Christians were only a generation away.

As the gospel was passed on from generation to generation, it often lost some of its original clarity and power. Sooner or later, the Lord would send prophets and teachers to bring revival and reformation to the church, which caused it to conform more clearly to the original gospel. This has happened many times in history, with movements like the Reformation occurring.

More recently God has awakened and transformed millions of people by pouring out the Holy Spirit in the Pentecostal and Charismatic renewals. Whenever the Church conforms to the "master" version of the gospel that Jesus Christ preached, there is a resultant explosion of power and purpose.

We are now living in a period of crisis. Some have called it "a decade of destiny." The New Age Movement looms menacingly over the horizon and is attempting to seduce many with a false gospel. Its emphasis on crystals, channeling, diet, healing, homeopathic remedies, past lives, and the like is a poor counterfeit to the life found in Jesus Christ.

But as Christians begin conforming to the image of Jesus Christ through the life-changing power of the Holy Spirit and the authority of the Word, we are going to bring the healing flow of the blood of the Lamb to a deceived and dying generation. The New Age promises much, but ultimately it cannot deliver because it is not based on truth. Despite all of its talk about love and peace, the New Age Movement is built on the foundation of mythology rather than truth.

Millions of sincere believers around the world are coming to Jesus Christ in intercession and repentance, asking God to conform them to His original purpose for man and the church. As a consequence, the Lord is bringing His people into the full dimension of His power and purpose—the same power and purpose the New Testament Christians had, only with a spiritual mandate that is fresh for this hour.

> I pray that the eyes of your heart may be enlightened, so that you may know what is the hope of His calling, what are the riches of the glory of His inheritance in the saints, and what is the surpassing greatness of His power toward us who believe—Ephesians 1:18-19.

Satan may think he has stolen the rainbow, but it is still ours—God has promised us abundant life in Christ. The way we become all that God created us to be is to have faith in Him and His mighty power. Supernatural faith is the key that releases the full power and glory of His presence in our generation.

CHAPTER THREE

A Thirst For Truth

Unlike most of the people who suggest that certain Bible teachers and evangelists are expounding doctrines that stem from the New Age Movement, I have had direct experience with the *NAM*. In other words, I did not study the *NAM* from afar—I was extensively involved in its practices for over a decade until the love of Jesus Christ rescued me from this deception.

My spiritual pilgrimage began at a very young age when the questions, "Who am I?" "What is my purpose in life?" and "What am I doing here?" haunted me and burned in my mind night and day. While other children were content to play, I was driven to ask questions about the meaning of life. Raised in New York City, I came from a liberal, educated family. Both my parents were teachers, and neither believed in God.

As a young boy, I thought science could give me the answers to my questions about life. Reading every book I could get my hands on about science and the lives of the great scientists, I often devoured ten books a week. I read about men like Albert Einstein, Nicola Tesla, Thomas Edison, Enrico Fermi, Louis Pasteur, and John Oppenheimer. Building a huge laboratory in my bedroom, I undertook amateur experiments on cryogenics and nuclear physics. Soon, however, I realized that these brilliant men did not have the answers I was looking for. Thus, at an early age I discovered the bankruptcy of scientific materialism.

After exhausting science as a means of finding the meaning of life, I next investigated the occult and Eastern religions. Biblical Christianity was not even an option for me. I had never once met a Bible-believing Christian or seen an evangelist on television, and the churches in my neighborhood were steeped in liberal theology or dead orthodoxy.

Due to my grandmother's influence, I did attend religious instruction at a local Catholic school once a week. I felt like a character from a Woody Allen movie, however, and questioned the nuns about their faith with malicious skepticism. One day the nun told us that a person would go to hell if they did not confess Jesus as their Savior. I asked her what would happen if a soldier in a war decided to accept Jesus Christ but was unable to make this confession because he had been shot in the throat. Would he go to hell? Grabbing me by the arm, she took me to the priest's office, where I was disciplined for being a "troublemaker."

The streets of New York City were a battleground, and the tough Irish boys who attended Catholic school often started fights with the public school kids. One afternoon a group of them cornered me and asked if I was Catholic. My parents told me to tell people we were "existentialists," so that was how I responded. They proceeded to pound me to an existential pulp. This was my first experience at being "evangelized" by a "Bible-believing" Christian.

I don't relate this to come down on Catholics, for I know many who love the Lord with all their heart. But my early experiences with "Christians" of all denominations convinced me that Christianity was spiritually bankrupt.

Consequently, I began reading books by men like Edgar Cayce and other occult writers. Soon I started practicing meditation and putting myself in trances. At the ripe old age of twelve, I was desperate to find answers to my spiritual questions.

The only religion we had at home was secular humanism—the belief that there is no God and man is the center of the universe. As a result, I was raised to believe that there was no absolute right or wrong. Around the dinner table, my parents taught me that human evil was due to ignorance and that the concept of a personal God was an archaic belief any educated person should transcend. In addition, they told me that Christians were intellectually pathetic people who were "anti-love," "anti-joy," and "anti-sex." Instead of promoting anything good, Christians were responsible for the crusades and the Inquisition.

One Thanksgiving evening, my grandmother asked my father to pray. Instead, he launched into a thunderous tirade about how there was no reason to thank God—everything we had came from man's hard work.

When family friends came to visit, my father, who was an artist, would discuss the philosophy of Friedrich Nietzsche and Jean Paul Sartre, as well as art and culture. Thankfully, many years later my father prayed a prayer of deliverance from alcoholism and became a Christian. Today he is a faithful believer in Jesus Christ.

Psychotherapy And Psychedelia

In the atheistic environment of my home, the spiritual void within me grew deeper, and I plunged headlong into *NAM* philosophy and radical politics. Soon after I reached puberty, my parents divorced, ripping my world apart. My spiritual pilgrimage merged with a growing hatred of all authority and society. I was ripe to be seduced by the counterculture and the psychedelic philosophy of the sixties, which has now become the New Age Movement.

Although my mother held a secular humanist world view, she was always full of loving concern and discipline. She spent thousands of hours reading me books and taking me to museums and libraries. Genuinely concerned about her rebellious son, my mother sent me to a psychotherapist whom she hoped would solve my problems.

I told my therapist that I wanted to know why I was alive, who I was, and what purpose there was for my life. He could not help me and only provided a listening board. In the vain hope of finding answers, I began reading Sigmund Freud, Carl Rogers, and Carl Jung. But all the leading psychological theorists seemed to contradict each other, and I was left more confused than ever.

Then the "hippie" movement with its drugs and "free love" exploded across the nation. I remember the first time I saw Timothy Leary. Wearing a white outfit and grinning like the "Cheshire Cat" from *Alice In Wonderland*, he said on national television "Tune in, turn on, and drop out." This psychedelic prophet of LSD was in distinct contrast to the people involved in organized religion. Then the Beatles recorded "*Sgt. Peppers Lonely Hearts Club Band*," and the psychedelic invasion of drugs, Eastern religion, and promiscuous sex spread.

At the age of fifteen, I was wearing long hair and boots and demonstrating with Abbie Hoffman in New York City. I organized demonstrations and was even made an honorary member of the Black Panther Party for protesting outside a prison against the arrest of Panther leaders.

Simultaneously, I deepened my activities in Eastern mysticism and was introduced to drugs by an "honor student" in my high school. I read a book by Aldous

Huxley titled *Heaven and Hell and the Doors of Perception*, which describes Huxley's experimentation with hashish and mescaline as a means to enter a higher state of consciousness. This fellow student, whose father was a doctor, "turned me on" to hashish and mescaline as part of a serious scientific experiment. Together, we passed through the "doors of perception" and entered a higher realm of consciousness.

William James, the respected American psychologist, said,

> Our normal waking consciousness is but one special type of consciousness: whilst all about it, parted from it by the filmiest screens there lies a potential form of consciousness entirely different . . . No account of the universe in its totality can be final which leaves these other forms of consciousness quite disregarded.[1]

James stressed that the existence of other forms of consciousness "forbid the premature closing of our accounts with reality." It is this belief system that lays the groundwork for the *NAM* and has influenced New Age pioneers like Jane Roberts, the founder of Aspect Psychology, and Dr. John C. Lilly.

Actress Shirley MacLaine had this to say about this other "reality" in a *Los Angeles Times* article:

> The West has given mankind science and technology but the East is influencing a return to man's spiritual heritage. The focus is on knowing that our unseen internal reality is just as important to our well-being as that which is visible.[2]

Fueled by drugs like LSD and mescaline, it was the psychedelic sixties that ushered in the current New Age Movement. Powerful mind altering drugs like LSD blasted people into the spiritual realm and forced them to acknowledge the presence of a spiritual reality. This opened the door to the occult and the myriad practices of Eastern mysticism that gave birth to the *NAM*.

Dr. John C. Lilly, the scientist responsible for the breakthroughs regarding the intelligence of dolphins, also introduced the "deep tank" as a means of consciousness expansion. If you research his work, you will see a common thread of experimentation with psychedelic drugs preceding emergence into New Age philosophy.

In my own life, the use of powerful psychedelic drugs like LSD intensified my plunge into *NAM* philosophy and Eastern mysticism. Thus began an electric pilgrimage into Hinduism, Buddhism, the teachings of Don Juan, yoga, mental telepathy, altered states of consciousness, hypnotherapy, astral projection, reincarnation, the occult, devil's weed, spirit guides, and a smorgasbord of mystical experiences. I was greatly influenced by men like Baba Ram Dass, Ken Kesey, Timothy Leary, and Stephen Gaskin.

In fact, my major at the University of Missouri was called "Altered States of Consciousness," a brand-new accredited field within the Department of Psychology. We studied different means of entering higher states of consciousness and engaged in exercises based on Eastern mystical teaching and experiences by men like Carlos Castaneda. It was during this time of intense New Age activity that I developed spiritual powers and "cosmic consciousness."

My professor at the University of Missouri was a practicing mystic and taught a number of courses on mental illness. He believed, as did popular psychologists like R. D. Laing, that mental illness or madness could be a means of entering higher consciousness. In this theory, insane people are considered spiritual pilgrims caught between two realities.

My professor invited gurus to teach and perform supernatural feats of levitation. Once while my professor was lecturing, I heard a distinct voice within me shout, "Surrender to the dark forces within!" At this point in my life I noticed a growing intensity in the manifestation of strong paranormal experiences. Yet at the same time, I had a growing feeling that things were getting out of control. The more bizarre things became, however, the more I believed I was moving toward "enlightenment." I became convinced that everything happening was due to my excess "karma" burning off.

As is often the case with people involved in drugs and the occult, I experienced mixed feelings of great elation and depression. I became a kind of mystical "wildman," hiking into the woods while on psychedelic drugs and communing with what I thought was God. But I was like a comet crashing into the atmosphere, burning more brightly as I moved through the heavens and consuming myself in flames. One evening I broke into my psychology professor's office and wrote him an anonymous note warning him of the dangers of "the journey."

Invasion Of The Jesus Movement

In the early seventies, a strange thing began to happen at the University of Missouri: The Jesus Movement spread from the West Coast and entered the campus town of Columbia, Missouri. I remember seeing an article on the Jesus Movement in a national magazine. Reading about these Christians, who I thought were going to regress mankind into a new dark age with their "primitive blood-stained religion,'' made me furious. I hated them because I thought they would stop the "revolution" and the establishment of the new world order based on higher consciousness.

People involved in the New Age Movement hold the very same beliefs, for their goal is to create a one-world government and unify the planet under a spiritual system of higher consciousness. Like many New Agers, I viewed Christians with all their talk of Jesus Christ being the "only way" as an anachronism and a threat to the spiritual-political revolution coming to the planet.

About this time, however, I finally came face to face with genuine Christians who moved in the supernatural flow of the Holy Spirit and had the glory of God shining on their countenances. I encountered Spirit-filled Christians everywhere and, like Saul of Tarsus, thought it was my duty to defend the faith of Eastern mysticism and the religion of "higher consciousness." Attacking and debating believers in philosophy classes whenever they spoke out about their faith, I delighted in trying to humiliate them and prove them wrong through intellectual arguments.

In addition, I increased my "outrageous" behavior in front of Christians in an attempt to mock and ridicule them. Since I studied film, I made X-rated animation movies with Barbie dolls in an attempt to sneer at Judeo-Christian morality.

Despite my bitter hatred, a couple of true Christians began to zero in on me and share the love of Jesus Christ. Beneath all my bravado was a hurting, frightened individual reaching out for answers. At first, my mind completely rejected everything they were saying. But they continued to love me with a pure, deep, spiritual *agape* love. Even though I thought what they were saying was complete idiocy, I felt myself being wooed and convicted by the Holy Spirit as they talked.

For the first time in my life, I sensed God's love for me. All my intellectual arguments were reduced to nothing as I encountered something far more real than anything I had experienced before. This was not some "trip" or mystical high. The purity and love that I felt *had* to be God.

Empowered by the Holy Spirit, these supernatural Christians opened up their lives to me. They cared about me as a person and loved me. They invited me to their prayer meetings and had me over for dinner. Through their personal ministry to me, I felt the arms of the living God embrace me and hug me like my father never had. As the Lord touched me deep within my heart, the hurt and bruised child locked inside me emerged and responded to His love.

Although I wasn't yet ready to surrender, the Holy Spirit continued to work in my life. I had all kinds of intellectual questions, so my Christian friends gave me a book by Dr. Francis Schaeffer called *Escape From Reason*. It changed my life. I was shocked to discover that a person could be both intelligent and a Christian. Talking about God, film, art, and philosophy in brilliant and articulate terms, Dr. Schaeffer explained contemporary culture in a way I had never understood.

Still I fought with the Holy Spirit, and the forces of darkness did not want to let me go. As these Christians prayed for me, the Holy Spirit continued to convict me. Sometimes I found myself walking alone by the highway, and, even though I was "stoned," I would begin sobbing and weeping as Almighty God touched me.

The Hand Of Providence

One afternoon a guy named Tim invited me to a retreat in a wooded area about an hour away from the campus. I had mysteriously met Tim in the hallway of a dormitory, where he sat reading the Bible that he carried with him everywhere. He was in the hallway to meet someone else, but providentially he met me and invited me to this Christian retreat. Tim's eyes shone with sincerity and the love of God, so I accepted his invitation.

Dressed in boots, blue jeans, and long hair, I arrived at the retreat center. A brief look at the place quickly convinced me that these people didn't have what I was looking for. They were the kind of Christians I had seen before—religious but lacking the depth and dimension of people who have had a personal encounter with Jesus Christ.

While at the retreat center, I noted vague references to the Bible, but primarily we played games like "spin the bottle." I was totally disgusted, for these people reinforced my worst preconceptions about Christianity. After spending the night, I told Tim during breakfast that I was going to hitchhike back to the university. Tim walked me to the highway and said, "Paul, God will take care of your ride home." Wondering if he was some kind of religious nut but hoping to humor him, I said, "Yeah, yeah sure." Then I stuck out my thumb and tried to hitch a ride.

The first person to pick me up was a Pentecostal preacher. He and his wife talked to me about Jesus the entire ride. Stunned, I chalked it up as coincidence; after all, this *was* the Bible Belt. After they let me out, I stuck out my thumb and was picked up by a Bible salesman with a station wagon filled with Bibles! As we whizzed down the highway, he opened a giant Bible and began reading. With no hands on the wheel, he asked me if I wanted to receive Jesus into my life. I managed to gulp a "yes," and he pulled off the road.

As we rolled to a stop, the thought raced through my mind, What have I got myself into? Is this guy some kind of religious psychopath or axe murderer? Growing up in New York City had taught me to suspect everybody's motives and not to trust strangers.

The next thing I knew this Bible salesman was leading me in a prayer. With head bowed and hands clasped, I heard myself saying, "Jesus Christ, I ask you to forgive me of my sins. I invite you to come into my life and make me born again. In Jesus' name. Amen." I couldn't believe I had said this prayer. I wasn't even sure what sin was, although it seemed to me like an archaic concept. But I prayed in faith and meant it.

Hours later, I forgot the incident had even occurred and "partied" the night away with friends. The next day I woke up hung over and decided to visit a Christian girl named Laura. She and her boyfriend, Burgess, had spent a lot of time ministering and witnessing to me about Jesus.

As Laura and I talked, we were walking next to some giant Roman columns in the university quadrangle. I told her about my highway experience, and another girl sitting on the lawn overheard our conversation. It turned out that she was a minister's daughter wrestling with the question of whether or not Christianity was really true. Looking at me point-blank, she said, "Do you believe that Jesus Christ was the Son of God?"

All of a sudden the words, "Yes, I believe that Jesus Christ is the Son of God!" leapt from deep within me. I was shocked. I had never said anything like that before. As I spoke, I had the most powerful spiritual experience of my life. It seemed that the sky had cracked open, and the presence of God overwhelmed me. A giant veil was lifted from my eyes as I realized God truly did exist.

I understand that I risk losing credibility by relating this experience exactly as it happened. True miracles can be cheapened by relating them in either a glib or a sensational manner. Many Christians carelessly utter the word "mira-cle" with such arrogance that it loses all its value. In addition, I understand that many people have had quiet but profound experiences with Jesus Christ that have just as much validity as mine.

But for me to minimize or reduce what happened to more logical terms just to make it more plausible would be inaccurate. I felt as if every dream I had ever had within the depths of my soul came true in an instant. Literally caught up in the Holy Spirit, I felt I was floating for weeks. Although I was higher than I had ever been in my entire life, I knew that the experience was genuine and pure.

Everything I had searched for in Eastern mysticism, human relationships, and the New Age Movement I now found in Jesus Christ. This was not just another higher state of consciousness, an "upper story leap" without rational content, or a mystical trip. Nothing about this was artificial or mystical.

Connected to reality at a deeper dimension than I had ever experienced, my inner being and personality were shook to the core as I came face to face with the infinite God of the universe. If you have ever been in love with another person, the experience is but the smallest fraction of what a personal relationship with Jesus Christ is like. God's presence became more real to me than all the so-called tangible objects around me.

Truth—The Final Experience

There is a danger in the charismatic movement of becom-ing intoxicated with *experiences* of the Holy Spirit and somehow losing an anchor with God-given rationality and reason. God created the intellect and the ability to perceive and analyze. True Christianity and authentic experiences with the Holy Spirit do not occur apart from reason or applied intelligence.

Faith does not exist apart from reason because the Bible is true in *every* dimension of life—spiritual, scientific, historical, psychological, etc. This is the radical difference between Christianity and "religions." Unlike Hinduism, which is based on myth—the "Lord" Krishna never even existed in space-time history, and the many Hindu gods and deities are purely mythological—the Bible and accounts of the nation of Israel are rooted in history.

Archeological relics and written records support biblical accounts. In addition, all of the miracles in the Bible take place within the context of verifiable history. In other words, archaeologists and historians have *proof* of things like the resurrection of Jesus Christ, the crossing of the Red Sea, and the destruction of Jericho. Prophesies about future events that have been carefully recorded are fulfilled time and again. This is not true of New Age and Eastern mystical accounts, where fact and fiction are blended together with the distinctions hopelessly blurred.

I appreciate the position of those who look upon the supernatural dimension of life with suspicion—especially those who have heard so much empty talk about the miraculous that they have deafened their ears to all accounts of the present-day miracles of Jesus Christ. There has been a negative backwash to the current move of the Holy Spirit, and that is the glib, arrogant, and swaggering manner in which many genuine miracles have been communicated to the world. In addition, emotionalism, group hysteria, and exaggeration have been passed off as the work of the Holy Spirit. Nevertheless, Jesus Christ is still working miracles today in the lives of believers.

One could easily misconstrue my involvement in the *NAM* and my encounter with Jesus Christ as the path of someone hopping from experience to experience lacking rational and verifiable content. Let me assure you that when I began my spiritual journey I did so as a scientist and a skeptic.

The contrast between mystical experiences and my encounter with Jesus Christ was as different as night and day. All of the New Age and Eastern mystical experiences I was involved in had an illusory quality no matter how real they seemed at the time. Jesus Christ was not just another "experience." My newfound relationship with Him conveyed a reality so strong that *I knew that I knew* I had found God.

CHAPTER FOUR
The Source Of Power

The New Age Movement is not "new," and the spiritual beliefs held by its followers have been around since the days of ancient Babylon. Drugs, reincarnation, astrology, meditation, regression, clairvoyance, astral projection, altered states of consciousness, past lives, channeling, spirit-guides, etc. have been in existence for centuries.

The *NAM* is a blend of these philosophies and practices integrated with technology, pseudo-science, and contemporary psychology. In our post-Christian culture, the ideas of the *NAM* and Eastern mysticism have gradually infiltrated society. Modern psychology, politics, personal relationships, education, business, and the liberal church have all been affected. In fact, due to the direct influence of Eastern philosophy, our culture has an extremely naive view of evil. This is manifest in our inability to deal effectively with violent criminals or take decisive action against terrorists and militant Marxists.

The Spiritual Mother Of The New Age

The spiritual mother of the New Age Movement, as well as Eastern mysticism, Buddhism, and a number of other practices, is the ancient religion of Hinduism. The dabbler in *NAM* philosophy and other Eastern mystical practices would be stunned to discover that most techniques for "self realization" come right out of the Hindu "bible."

Hinduism came into prominence around 2000 B.C. through an ancient people called the *Aryans*. The *Aryans* practiced a religion of prayers, hymns, and chanting that was recorded in the *Vedic* literature. The *Vedas* give the Hindu an outline for life and has four stages: (1) *a student*; (2) *the head of the family*; (3) *a spiritual pilgrim* (who may live the life of a hermit); (4) *total renunciation of the things of this world*.

As Hinduism developed, the writings of what is termed the *Upanishads* were written somewhere between 800 and 300 B.C. The *Upanishads* teach the concept that man can attain a God-like consciousness called the *brahmanatman*, which is ultimate reality; life as we know it is considered *maya*, or illusion. The goal of Hinduism is to transcend *maya* by traveling through the four stages.

Eventually the *Bhagavad Gita* was written and became to good Vishnuites and most Hindus what the New Testament is to the Christian. The *Bhagavad Gita* has become a source of teaching for millions of Hindus. The central characters of this book, Krishna and Arjuna, are totally fictitious people. These mythical characters, who dominate the literature passed out by Hindu groups like the Hare Krishna Society, never even existed. This is in direct contrast to the Bible, which is built entirely on historical fact.

One of the major tenets of the Hindu religion is *punarjanman*, or reincarnation. A person's *atman,* or soul, supposedly journey's through a series of births and deaths, evolving into a higher state of order. This spiritual evolution is achieved by the Hindu devotee working out his karma through religious duties or *yoga*. In this concept, a person's soul eventually achieves God-consciousness and is said to have reached *nirvana*.

Contemplating Your Navel
With The Buddha

A direct offshoot of the Hindu religion is Buddhism. Buddhism was founded by Siddhartha Gautama who was born a Hindu around 56 B.C. in India. Siddhartha Gautama, later called the Buddha, spent his childhood years in a beautiful palace insulated from the tragedies of life.

One day while riding in the park just outside the palace walls, Siddhartha Gautama was shocked to discover the harsh realities of life. All around him he saw poverty, sickness, and death. Like many young people today, Siddhartha was not satisfied with the comforts of his upper class lifestyle and went on a spiritual quest.

Sporting a shaved head and a robe, Siddhartha Gautama wandered around the country looking for answers. Discontented with Hinduism, he experimented with a variety of approaches to God, which only led to further frustration. In desperation, he decided to meditate under a tree and, among other things, "contemplate his navel." After forty days, Siddhartha thought he had achieved *nirvana* and became known as the "Buddha" or the "enlightened one."

The Buddha's teaching, which evolved from the major tenets of Hinduism, basically says that all living involves a high degree of suffering. We must all experience this pain until we achieve *nirvana*. Like the Hindu, the Buddhist believes that each person must go through a series of reincarnations before reaching *nirvana* and becoming free of the wheel of birth and death.

Buddha taught a way to reach nirvana called "The Noble Eight-fold Path," consisting of eight techniques a person may employ to earn salvation. They are: (1) *right viewpoint*; (2) *right aspirations*; (3) *right speech*; (4) *right behavior*;

(5) *right occupation*; (6) *right effort*; (7) *right mindfulness*; (8) *right meditation*. The Buddha's teachings are a rigorous program of self-improvement. Like its predecessor, Hinduism, however, Buddhism is in direct contradiction to the Bible on many points.

The Bible says "all our righteousnesses are as filthy rags" (Isaiah 64:6, *KJV*). What this means is that *no* amount of self-righteousness can please God and earn salvation. In other words, all of man's attempts to purify himself are like "filthy rags" before God. The Lord is not on a power trip; it's just that self-effort cannot bridge the massive gap between a holy, pure God and sinful man.

Since it is impossible for man to earn his way to salvation and heaven, then there must be another way. The apostle Paul explains the Lord's method of salvation in Ephesians 2:8-9: "For by grace you have been saved through faith; and not of yourselves, it is the gift of God; not as a result of works, that no one should boast." The word grace means "unmerited favor"—favor that is not based on performance or self-effort.

This is what distinguishes Christianity from every other religion or spiritual belief system in the world. According to the Bible, absolutely nothing a person can do will earn him salvation. All God requires is our willingness to accept His free gift of salvation in Jesus Christ.

Turning To The East For Answers

Hinduism, Buddhism, Eastern mysticism, and other New Age-type philosophies did not have any effect on our culture until the 1950s. Until that time, the predominate world view of the West was the Judeo-Christian ethos. Several important historical trends merged during that period, creating a spiritual vacuum in Western culture that made it ripe for seduction by Eastern mystical philosophies.

First, we had the expansion of a theologically liberal Christian church and the subsequent expansion of the dual philosophies of scientific materialism and secular humanism. A quick view of the science fiction movies from the 1950s reveals a false faith in science and technology to solve mankind's problems. The optimism of the 1950s was shattered by the assassination of John F. Kennedy, the war in Vietnam, and a growing spiritual emptiness—partially created by a Christian church that did not provide answers or meaning.

In his book, *The Dust Of Death*, Os Guinness writes,

> The swing to the East has come at a time when Christianity is weak at just those points where it would need to be strong to withstand the East. . . . Modern Christianity is crucially weak at three vital points. The first is a compromised, deficient understanding of revelation. Without Biblical historicity and veracity behind the Word of God, theology can only grow closer to Hinduism. Second, the modern Christian is drastically weak in an unmediated, personal, experiential knowledge of God. Often what passes for religious experience is a communal emotion felt in church services, in meetings, in singing or contrived fellowship. Few Christians would know God on their own. Third, the modern church is often pathetically feeble in the expression of its focal principle of community.[1]

Mr. Guinness grasps the crisis of the Christian church, which is being assaulted by Eastern mystical and New Age philosophies. I would add to his analysis, however, a fourth weakness of the modern Christian Church—the lack of supernatural power that Jesus Christ said His followers should have.

Unfortunately, contemporary Christian culture has succumbed to two problems in this area. One is a *disbelief* in the miraculous flow of the supernatural power of the Holy Spirit through the lives of believers. The other is an *overemphasis* on the supernatural power of God with an accompanying anti-intellectualism, experience-based Christianity and a pervasive lack of integrity in using the gifts of the Holy Spirit. These two extremes created a spiritual vacuum in our culture that Eastern-based religions and *NAM* philosophies have rushed in to fill.

In the 1950s and early 1960s, a counterculture that embraced Hinduism, Buddhism, and Eastern mystical beliefs started to emerge. In addition, this counterculture rejected Judeo-Christian morality and began a sexual revolution and the widespread use of drugs. Krishnamurti, Maharishi Mahesh Yogi, Meher Baba, Yogananda, D.T. Suzuki, Allen Ginsberg, Aldous Huxley, Ken Kesey, Timothy Leary, Alan Watts, Jack Kerouac, and others ushered in an Eastern mystical-chemical counterculture that in the 1980s has become the New Age Movement.

LSD And The Deep Tank

Serious scientists like Dr. John C. Lilly took this blend of Eastern mystical ideas based on Hinduism and Buddhism along with psychedelic drugs and helped prepare the intellectual groundwork for the *NAM*. Dr. Lilly is famous for announcing to the world that dolphins are possibly as intelligent as human beings. He is a scientist, psychoanalyst, and a doctor of medicine with credentials in neurophysiology, biophysics, electronics, and neuroanatomy.

Dr. Lilly is also a pioneer in the "new consciousness movement," which is the New Age belief that man is capable of solving all of his problems through consciousness expansion. Experimenting with LSD, which altered his state of consciousness and caused him to acknowledge the spiritual dimension of reality, Lilly devoted his life to understanding higher consciousness. He worked extensively with the Easlen Institute in Big Sur, California, and Oscar Ichazo's Arica Institute.

In his classic experiment with sensory deprivation in a deep tank with LSD, Dr. Lilly chartered new worlds in the field of parapsychology. For years, psychologists have induced hallucinations in patients through a process called sensory deprivation. All that is needed is for a person to be shut off in a darkened room with no sound or other sense stimuli for several days. As a result of having his senses deprived of normal stimuli, a person in this environment will begin to experience hallucinations. Dr. Lilly amplified this process by using a "deep tank" and combining it with LSD.

The deep tank is a pool of body-temperature water in which a person is submerged. No light, sound, or smell is allowed in, and the subject is given a dose of LSD. The synergistic effect of these combined forces is that the hallucinations will increase exponentially.

Using himself as his subject, Dr. Lilly would submerge himself in a deep tank while ingesting large amounts of LSD. When he combined this powerful drug with the deep tank, Lilly found that he could literally blast his consciousness out of his body. Soon he began regularly traveling through many different dimensions.

On one particular occasion, Lilly was traveling through inner space when he came into a place of great brilliant light and warmth. As he entered this dimension of golden light, he encountered two "guides," who began communicating with him. They gave him specific instructions about how to find the answers he was looking for. As a result of these experiments, Dr. Lilly came up with the concept of the human mind as a great "biocomputer" that can be programmed to live in a higher state of consciousness. He outlines these states as *"+48, +24, +12, +6, and +3."* The *"+3"* state is the level of consciousness where one supposedly reaches *satori*, or enlightenment.

John C. Lilly is one of the founding fathers of the New Age Movement. He teaches techniques of exploring inner space through diet, meditation, drugs, and self-awareness exercises. At the core of his work is this fundamental belief, which articulates the hope of the *NAM*:

> What one believes to be true is either true or becomes true within the limits to be found experientially or experimentally. These limits are beliefs to be transcended. . . . It is my firm belief that the experience of higher states of consciousness is necessary for the survival of the human species.[2]

As a former veteran of inner-space travel who has logged thousands of hours of "flight" into realms of higher consciousness, I know that what happened to Dr. Lilly is real. Many people involved in the *NAM* are experiencing these kind of things.

I was unable to afford the expensive technology of a large deep tank with an insulated room and heating unit. Instead, I would take a large dose of LSD, go into a dark bathroom, relax in a tub of body-temperature water, and meditate for hours in total silence. In this simulated deep-tank experience, and by taking hallucinogenic drugs, I was able to blast into higher states of consciousness and communicate with "spirit guides." Although I could not see these beings, I was very aware that they were there and could converse with them while in a hallucinatory state.

All of this happened prior to accepting Jesus Christ as my Lord and Savior. I did not understand that there was a spiritual war going on and that the "spirit guides" I was talking to were actually demons. Lucifer is a powerful spiritual being in open rebellion against God. His plan is to seduce mankind through "signs" and "false wonders."

> . . . that is, the one whose coming is in accord with the activity of Satan, with all power and false wonders—2 Thessalonians 2:9.

> Children, it is the last hour; and just as you heard that the anti-christ is coming, even now many anti-christs have arisen; from this we know that it is the last hour. . . . Who is the liar but the one who denies that Jesus is Christ? This is the anti-christ, the one who denies the Father and the Son—1 John 2:18, 22.

Spirit Guides Or Personal Demons?

Another pioneer in the New Age Movement is Jane Roberts. She has developed a whole new branch of psychology called "Aspect Psychology," which explores precognitive dreams, astral projection, revelatory information, consciousness-changing techniques, peak experiences, trance mediumship, and other parapsychological events. Like many other proponents of the *NAM*, Roberts firmly believes that our consciousness is mobile and that we can enter different realities at will.

While playing with a ouija board in 1963, Jane and her husband reportedly contacted a personality from another dimension. The personality introduced himself as "Seth" and began communicating detailed messages. Soon Jane Roberts began passing into a trance, allowing Seth's voice to speak through her. As a seasoned medium, Roberts actively encourages the use of ouija boards, telepathy, automatic writing, and seances. She leads classes in "Aspect Psychology," in which "long robed spirit beings" come into the room and communicate with different members of the class.

In her books, Jane Roberts states that she does not believe in good spirits and bad spirits, demons, possession, or the power of evil as they're generally described in Christian thought. This viewpoint is crucial and pivotal, for Roberts obviously rejects God's Word. The Bible clearly indicates that Satan, demons, evil spirits, and possession are a reality. In fact, Jesus Christ "went about doing good, and healing all those who were oppressed by the devil" (Acts 10:38). How could He go about doing good and healing all those who were oppressed by the devil unless there was a devil? The Lord also cast demons out of people. How could Jesus cast demons out unless demons could oppress and possess people?

As for the practice of mediumship, Leviticus 20:27 says, "Now a man or a woman who is a medium or a spiritist shall surely be put to death. They shall be stoned with stones, their bloodguiltiness is upon them." Clearly, the practice of mediumship, or what is now popularly called "channeling," was considered a serious offense against God by the Old Testament prophets.

The apostle Paul also had some strong words to say about someone who was involved in the "Aspect Psychology" of his day. He didn't have a long theological debate with the person; he merely demonstrated the full authority and supernatural power of a true believer in Jesus Christ:

> And it happened that as we were going to the place of prayer, a certain slave-girl having a spirit of divination met us, who was bringing her masters much profit by fortune telling. Following after Paul and us, she kept crying out and saying, "These men are bond-servants of the Most High God, who are proclaiming to you a way of salvation." And she continued doing this for many days. But Paul was greatly annoyed, and turned and said to the spirit, "I command you in the name of Jesus Christ come out of her!" And it came out at that very moment—Acts 16:16-18.

The struggle between biblical Christianity and the New Age Movement is not a battle between two equally good ideas. One is truth and the other is deception. The apostle Paul did exactly what a modern faith teacher would do. He said, "I command you in the name of Jesus Christ come out of her!" He spoke the Word of God with authority and ordered the demonic spirit to go.

This was the Word of God and obedience to Jesus Christ's command to preach the "gospel of the kingdom" and "cast out demons" being confirmed with "signs and wonders." Paul didn't try to explain away the supernatural with humanistic explanations. He spoke the Word of God and took authority over the situation. His words and actions were a precise capsulization of what contemporary faith teaching is all about. It is interesting to note that the occult spirit within the girl was also attempting to lie and deceive the people who were watching by performing supernatural acts of divination.

The Sorcerer's Apprentice

Still another contributor to current New Age philosophy is Carlos Castaneda, who wrote *The Teaching of Don Juan: A Yaqui Way of Knowledge.* In 1960 Castaneda, a student at the University of California in Los Angeles, went to the Southwest to collect information on medicinal plants used by the Indians. He claimed that he had encountered a Yaqui Indian from Sonora, Mexico, named Don Juan. This Indian reputedly had the "secret knowledge" and was a *brujo,* which is Spanish for medicine man, curer, witch, and sorcerer. The word connotes a person with extraordinary and unusually evil powers.

Castaneda became an apprentice of Don Juan from June, 1961, until September, 1965, in Arizona and Sonora, Mexico. During that time, Don Juan led Carlos into different realities and the "moment of twilight" through the use of mescaline, *yerba del diablo* (herb of the devil), and peyote. Don Juan received his teaching from a *diablero,* which in the language of the Sonoran Indians means an evil person who practices black sorcery and is capable of transforming himself into an animal.

Like John C. Lilly and other New Age proponents, Don Juan believed that states of non-ordinary reality or altered states of consciousness were the only form of pragmatic learning and the way to acquire a spirit guide, or "ally." The purpose of Don Juan's teaching was to help Castaneda acquire an "ally" through drugs. Once again, we see mind-altering drugs being used to affect a person's state of consciousness and place him or her in a spiritual dimension where they are under the control and influence of demons.

While at the University of Missouri, at the request of my professor, my class practiced some of the teachings of Don Juan. Our first assignment was to find our own personal power spot or *sitio*. Over one hundred students from the "Altered States of Consciousness" class wandered all over this midwestern college town practicing Yaqui Indian sorcery and deliberately yielding our minds to suggestions from the spirit world. To supplement my college studies, I managed to buy some devil's weed and smoke it to increase my ability to enter a higher realm and acquire an "ally."

When the preacher's daughter, whom I mentioned earlier, confronted me and I finally confessed that Jesus Christ was the Son of God, I did it where my power spot or *sitio* was located—under the large Roman columns on the university quadrangle. There is absolutely no relationship between these demonic activities and my personal encounter with the living God, for spiritism and Christianity move an individual in radically different directions. I do believe, however, that God was trying to make a statement to me.

Like most people in the *NAM* I was looking for power and a means of controlling the circumstances in my life. Only Jesus Christ, the true God, has the power and authority over life. He was trying to show me that He alone is the Power. All my spiritual activities in the New Age left me spiritually bankrupt. But when I confessed Jesus Christ as Lord, I discovered that He was the answer to everything. God was telling me my "power spot" can only be found in Jesus Christ.

CHAPTER FIVE

Highway To Hell

Before finding the Lord Jesus Christ, I lived a life of total deception. I had plunged into the New Age Movement headfirst and was moving deeper and deeper into spiritual darkness; all the while I thought I was on the verge of enlightenment. This is the devil's game plan—to make you think you're on the right track when in reality you're moving in the opposite direction. In the next few pages I will share some experiences that woke me up to the fact that the New Age Movement is a dangerous and deadly lie.

Let me state right at the outset that whatever a person may be involved in—gurus, meditation, mind-altering drugs, horoscopes, Ouija Boards, channeling, Est, Lifespring, Freudian psychotherapy, regression, crystals, holistic healing, yoga, Christian Science, Unity, religious science, zen, Buddhism, or spaghetti and meatballs—it is wrong if it moves them away from a personal relationship with Jesus Christ.

I have been there. I tried practically everything before accepting Jesus Christ. Thankfully, the loving God of the universe set up some roadblocks and stop signs along the way; otherwise, I would probably be dead.

Warning Signs Along The Road

My first warning appeared late one evening when I was tripping on LSD and had gone from Central Park to stay over at my girlfriend's house in Queens. Her parents were both psychotherapists and were loving, nice people. They allowed me to stay in the maid's bedroom when she was not there.

Everyone else had gone to bed, and I was still awake hallucinating in a dark room. In fact, although the electric lights were all turned off, the room was stroboscoping brilliant flashes of light. In addition, hundreds of R. Crumb cartoon characters were running up and down the walls hollering gibberish and banging each other over the head with pots and pans.

After many hours of these hallucinations, I was afraid I would never come down off the LSD and was going to go permanently crazy and live in "Disneyland" the rest of my life. Looking over on a desk in the corner of the room, I saw a little picture postcard of Jesus Christ. I picked up the postcard and studied His face.

As I looked at the picture of the Son of God, it became apparent what I should do. It didn't matter that I was Mr. "Cosmic Voyager." When you're in trouble, you get honest quickly. So I got down on my hands and knees and prayed to Jesus Christ and asked Him to bring me down from my bad LSD trip. I asked Him to forgive me for all sorts of things and promised to give up smoking, drugs, and fooling around. Mysteriously, I came down off the LSD moments later and went to sleep. But I didn't keep my promise to God and kept heading down the path to destruction.

Filled with the foolishness of youthful rebellion, I continued in my pursuit of higher consciousness, spending a lot of time in the East Village on St. Mark's Place "dropping acid" and demonstrating with the Yippies. One day while on LSD I called my girlfriend from a pay phone. As we were talking, the phone in my hand began to melt and turn to rubber. Then my girlfriend's voice sounded like Minnie Mouse echoing "Hello, hello, hello." Next I heard a loud high-pitched squeal and jumped out of the phone booth to watch it melt on the sidewalk.

Taking LSD on a New York subway train was no joyride, either. Just as the train started to go through a tunnel under the Hudson River into Manhattan, peoples' faces suddenly began to melt and contort like grotesque figures in a burning wax museum. A blind man walked by with a seeing eye dog begging for money, and I began to hear shrieking and moaning as the subway went underground. I felt as if I was on a train bound for hell.

Although the experience was apparently purely hallucinatory, I believe that God was speaking to me about the direction of my life. I am not suggesting that people should take LSD to hear from God. What I am saying, however, is that in my total ignorance I was trying to find God by using LSD. I believe God spoke to me during those times because deep inside I was looking for Him even though I was looking in the wrong direction. Remember, I had never once met a Bible-believing Christian, and nobody had ever shared the gospel with me.

Face-To-Face With A Guru

While I was attending the University of Missouri, a famous guru named Stephen Gaskin came to campus. He was a former teacher with the California school system during the beginning of the Haight Ashbury hippie movement in San Francisco. Stephen became involved in the psychedelic world of mysticism and mind-altering drugs, which rocketed him, like others, into the world of the supernatural.

Stephen Gaskin began teaching a famous "Saturday Night Class," where large numbers of hippies, intellectuals, and spiritual pilgrims would gather. Together they meditated and practiced many of the consciousness-altering exercises that are the staples of the current New Age Movement. While the Flower Children in Haight Ashbury turned to guns and heroin, Stephen and his followers organized a large caravan of Greyhound buses with bright colored "mandalas" painted on them and left San Francisco in a psychedelic version of the exodus. They purchased a large farm in Tennessee and established a successful spiritual commune.

I had been reading Stephen Gaskin's books religiously. They described an assortment of New Age activities that I practiced—mental telepathy, higher consciousness, and going up on the astral plane. Stephen and the members of his commune came to the University of Missouri to give a lecture on higher consciousness, and I had the opportunity to talk with him after the seminar.

As Stephen and I were talking face to face, a strange thing began to happen to me: I felt like warm electrical fingers were massaging the inside of my mind. It seemed as if the spiritual force inside of Stephen was trying to enter my mind and communicate with me on a telepathic level. As this strong spiritual force came over me, I knew that I had a choice of whether or not to yield to it and let it in my mind.

As Stephen was looking at me in the typical serene manner of a guru, I suddenly had a strong inner sense that something was definitely wrong. Looking at him point blank, I said, "There's something wrong here! Something tells me I shouldn't trust you, and I will not let you enter my mind!"

Stephen looked at me with a puzzled expression, smiled, and then said, "We will meet again."

The encounter I had with Stephen Gaskin is typical of the encounters many people have with gurus. Spiritual

manifestations can occur in the presence of a guru or someone deeply involved in the *NAM* or the occult. When
people visit gurus or "enlightened" teachers, they
experience supernatural phenomenon like mental telepathy,
blissful states, feelings of peace, and strong manifestations
of the spiritual world. Sometimes gurus put their thumb or
fingers on the foreheads of their followers, and the people
receive a vision of inner light and are filled with an energy.
This is a Satanic counterfeit of the Baptism of the Holy Spirit.

Although these experiences are quite real, they are not
signs from God. Experience alone is not a sign from God.
*A supernatural experience must be in accordance with the
Scriptures in order for it to be of the Lord.* In other words,
supernatural phenomenon in and of themselves—miracles,
signs and wonders, spirits, etc.—do not prove that this
person or that guru is from God. The Bible warns of
deceiving signs and wonders and counterfeits to the work
of the Holy Spirit, and this is exactly what these things are.

We Are God's Roadblocks

When I met with Stephen Gaskin, my inner conviction
that "something is wrong" came from the Holy Spirit. Even
though I did not know Him, Jesus Christ in His love threw
up a stop sign to protect me. He is doing the same for
people involved in the New Age. If they are honest, they
will admit that certain urgings and promptings have told
them that what they are doing is not from God.

The Lord of the universe does not allow people to walk
to hell uninterrupted. He throws up roadblocks along the
way, sends prophets, and does everything in His power to
warn them. If you read carefully some of the accounts of
people involved in the *NAM*, such as John C. Lilly and
Rennie Davis, you will see that they have been warned.

They constantly refer to Christian and biblical teachings, God, Jesus, judgment, and hell. Rennie Davis, a member of the Chicago-Eight Conspiracy Trial, heard a voice warning him that his guru was an antichrist; but at the time he chose to ignore it.

We must pray for the people involved in the New Age Movement. God is not going to allow them to march off into oblivion without a fight. He wants to use His people to reach them. Will we be faithful, or will we ignore God's mandate?

> Deliver those who are being taken away to death, and those who are staggering to slaughter, O hold them back. If you say, "See, we did not know this," does He not know it who weighs the hearts? And does He not know it who keeps your soul? And will He not render to man according to his work?—Proverbs 24:11-12.

CHAPTER SIX

The Importance Of Faith

We live in a world of crisis on both the global and personal level. On the international scene we see war, famine, and political upheaval. In our neighborhoods we witness divorce, loneliness, drug addiction, alcoholism, child abuse, poverty, unemployment, suicide, disease, and despair.

As Christians, we believe in the death and resurrection of Jesus Christ and that we have salvation through faith in Him. It is also our faith in Him that gives us the strength and resources to face the challenges of life. Our lives are to be lived in a moment-by-moment trust in His goodness and leading. God has given us abundant resources to deal with all our problems, from the major issues facing our generation to the "nitty-gritty" details of life.

Jesus Christ was not some "bozo" stumbling around Galilee in a wig with an English accent looking like an actor from a Monty Python movie. Neither was He the skinny little Jesus portrayed in so much Sunday school literature.

Jesus Christ was Almighty God, the Creator of the universe in human form. His birth, death, and resurrection were not cosmic accidents. The coming of Jesus Christ to this earth—conceived by the Holy Spirit and born of the Virgin Mary—was the single most important event in human history.

But when he had considered this, behold, an angel of the Lord appeared to him in a dream, saying, "Joseph, son of David, do not be afraid to take Mary as your wife; for that which has been conceived in her is of the Holy Spirit. And she will bear a Son; and you shall call His name Jesus, for it is He who will save His people from their sins"—Matthew 1:20-21.

The historical fact of the miraculous conception of Jesus Christ slams against the flow of secular humanist thought in our culture like a tidal wave. Educational and scientific institutions go to great lengths to ignore or explain away the historical reality of Jesus Christ's supernatural entrance into this world; but they reel under the impact of the personal testimonies of millions who claim to have been miraculously born again through the same Holy Spirit who impregnated the Virgin Mary.

Rebellion In The Sandbox

Secular humanists espousing quasi-socialist and mystical world views constantly rebel against God's divine authority and attack the Christian faith. Regardless of this attempt to subvert God's plan through radical New Age philosophy, however, Christianity continues to spread throughout the world. Radical feminists, gay rights activists, militant socialists, and *NAM* leaders try to pummel Christianity into submission through attacks by the mass media, political maneuvers, and organized censorship. But the truth of Christianity continues to gain acceptance by inquiring, intelligent people.

Radical activists have plotted; conspired against; and used magazines, television news coverage, the United States

Senate, and the Supreme Court to set up a new world order apart from and in open rebellion to the teachings of Jesus Christ. The leaders of this movement, which viciously opposes the Judeo-Christian world view, sneer at Christians and attempt to undermine the church's power at every level.

The battle for the control of our nation is being raged in courtrooms, classrooms, television networks, movie theatres, and political arenas. It is no accident that Congress is investigating the electronic church or that the IRS is moving against Christian organizations. Frank Zappa's rails against any attempt to clean up a rock 'n' roll music industry that infuses our youth with occult, rebellious, and sexual lyrics are deliberate and malicious.

These powerful forces, at work on both a spiritual and human level, have a specific hidden agenda—to eradicate the influence of Christianity from our nation. When Congress investigates the electronic church, the issue isn't concern over people's money. The real goal is political control, and they recognize Christians and the electronic church as an opposing force to their plans for world power.

We need to forgive, pray for, and love these people. Many of them do not know what they are doing and are merely motivated by the "spirit of this age." Until we found Jesus Christ, many of us were just like our opponents. We must resist the temptation to fight the battle merely on the human level and wage war in the heavenlies with praise, prayer, and intercession.

> For the weapons of our warfare are not of the flesh, but divinely powerful for the destruction of fortresses. We are destroying speculations and every lofty thing raised up against the knowledge of God, and we are taking every thought captive to the obedience of Christ—2 Corinthians 10:4-5.

As we confront a world system in open rebellion to God's laws, we must remember that our battle is spiritual as well as physical. When Joshua surrounded Jericho with the armies of Israel, he was preceded by priests, who carried the ark of the Lord and continually blew trumpets. At the proper time, the people lifted their voices with a "great shout" as the priests blew the trumpets. When they did, the walls of Jericho came tumbling down.

We, too, are engaged in a battle with the enemies of the Lord and must allow our intercession, praise, and worship to go before us to destroy the walls of their fortified cities. Despite man's open rebellion against the rule of God, what the Bible declares about Jesus Christ remains true.

> For by Him all things were created, both in the heavens and on earth, visible and invisible, whether thrones or dominions or rulers or authorities—all things have been created by Him and for Him—Colossians 1:16.

Our world is like a giant sandbox built by a loving father for his children. Some of the children play in the sandbox and are grateful to their father for building it. Others deny that he had anything to do with it, throw sand, and rebel while the father is away. Nevertheless, their rebellion takes place in the sandbox that their father has built for them whether or not they choose to acknowledge it.

What Is The Full Gospel?

All of our problems can be traced back to their historic origins in the Garden of Eden, where our ancestors chose to disobey God. As a result of this choice, sin and death entered the world. All sin has its root in the Fall. There is a direct correlation between political, sociological, medi-cal, and psychological problems and the spiritual degener-ation of the human race stemming from Adam and Eve's disobedience.

The good news of the gospel is that God did not leave us in this horrible predicament but sent His Son Jesus Christ to save all of mankind. Salvation, however, does not just involve a man's soul, although that is what much of contemporary evangelical Christianity teaches. It includes the body, soul, and spirit of man. This total salvation is what the New Testament preached and what the contemporary faith movement has emphasized.

In a nutshell, what the so-called "faith teachers" empha-size is that God is good and that He is the God of the *now*!" They preach that Jesus Christ is Lord and that He has the solution to any problem you may have.

In fact, it was the television evangelists like Rex Humbard, Bishop Fulton Sheen, Oral Roberts, Billy Graham, and Kathryn Kuhlman who made the message of Jesus Christ accessible to millions of people. These men and women brought the teachings of Christianity and the old time "camp meeting" into the homes of people across the world.

While theologians and seminaries complicated the message of Jesus Christ, these early television evangelists told people that God loved them and was intimately concerned about all aspects of their lives—including their health and wealth. It was Oral Roberts who popularized the second verse of Third John, which has been a cornerstone of modern day faith teaching: "Beloved, I wish above all things that thou mayest prosper and be in health, even as thy soul prospereth" (3 John 2, *KJV*). The first time I read this verse was in an Oral Roberts newsletter. I didn't believe the Bible actually said it until I looked it up.

At the time, most of the Christians attending my church were always talking about being "crucified" and relishing in their sufferings. They almost glorified their problems. People went to the prayer altar week after week, weeping and crying and "a moaning and a groaning" about God's heavy hand upon them. They were always "dying to self" or "dying to the flesh." God seemed to have a wonderful plan of *failure* for them so they could "learn something"—which, by the way, they never seemed to learn or could never explain!

I'm not saying that there isn't a time for crucifying the flesh or dying to self, but sooner or later the resurrection should come! It was in this environment that I first came into contact with books by Kenneth Hagin and discovered the joy of victory in Jesus Christ.

Many Christian leaders, especially the faith teachers, have been accused of preaching a "health and wealth gospel." When I first heard it, I could have used a little "health" and "wealth." Like it or not, this concept is essentially biblical, as the second chapter of Third John proves. One cannot come up with a solid biblical argument refuting the principle that God desires His people to be prosperous and in health. In addition, many verses in the Word support the idea. For example,

> And let them say continually, "The Lord be magnified, Who delights in the prosperity of His servant"—Psalm 35:27.

> And in whatever he does, he prospers—Psalm 1:3.

> Those who wait for the Lord, they will inherit the land . . . and will delight themselves in abundant prosperity—Psalm 37:9,11.

Then the Book of Joshua talks about the promises of God toward the one who reads the Word and meditates on it:

> "This book of the law shall not depart from your mouth, but you shall meditate on it day and night, so that you may be careful to do according to all that is written in it; for then you will make your way prosperous, and then you will have success"—Joshua 1:8.

The Bible clearly teaches the gospel of "prosperity and success." When God says, "The book of the law shall not depart from your mouth," He means you are to speak or confess the Word instead of unbelief or your problems. If we are going to study the Bible and use it as our final authority, then we have to be honest about what it says. Scripture teaches "confession," "success," and "prosperity," and it is our duty before God to accept these verses for what they are. We must not attempt to distort or spiritualize them.

Abuses Of God's Blessings

On the other hand, although the Bible clearly indicates that God delights in the prosperity of His people, man's carnal nature, or "flesh," is prone to idolatry. The critics of the faith movement often have valid arguments when they point to the arrogance, pride, and idolatry of some who preach a "health and wealth gospel." There *has* been superficiality within some quarters of the "full gospel" movement that has cheapened the message they preach. Several organizations have turned the supernatural ministry of Jesus Christ into a circus-like atmosphere.

As I stated in the Introduction, I disagree with the critics' accusations that many of the faith teachers have been

influenced by the *NAM*. But I do share their concern over
the way some Christians on television seem to trivialize their
conversations with God. I believe in and practice the gifts
of the Holy Spirit, but there is a vast difference between
God's communication with us and our own imaginations.
This is not an attempt to squelch the Holy Spirit; it is a
plea for maturity and discernment. We in the charismatic
movement are sometimes a little too familiar with the Lord.
I don't mean intimate—I mean *cocky*.

Nowhere are these abuses more disturbing and apparent
than in the area of fund raising. According to a recent
Gallup Poll, 40 percent of all Americans feel only some or
very little Christian fund raising is honest.[1] Obviously,
to claim to be reaching the world for the Lord is ludicrous
if statistics indicate that we are alienating people from
Jesus Christ.

Gordon Loux, president of Prison Fellowship International, said, "I think the whole health-and-welfare gospel
is anathema, because you just don't see it in the Scriptures.
It's the twentieth century's version of the sale of indul-
gences."[2] While I disagree with the idea that "prosperity"
is not found in Scripture, I think Mr. Loux has pinpointed
a real problem in calling attention to the materialism and
ugliness often associated with the preaching of prosperity.

In the same interview in *Christianity Today*, David Clark,
vice president of marketing for the Christian Broadcasting
Network, commented,

> There's a lot of evidence that serving God results
> in a kind of redemptive lift. Just look at the
> Wesley revival . . . and how it changed people's
> lives for the better—even financially. That's a lit-
> tle different . . . from saying, "Give me $500 and
> the Lord is going to give you $5,000 back."[3]

Tim Robertson, the son of Pat Robertson and now president of the Christian Broadcasting Network, was quoted as saying that he attributes half of CBN's budget shortfall to the combined effect of his father's presidential bid and the PTL scandal.[4]

The PTL Club episode is evidence of a desperately needed reform within the church and those who preach "prosperity." Many Christian leaders agree on this point, including Pat Robertson, who suggested that the Lord "is cleaning His house." The Bakkers exemplified the worst that could go wrong by emphasizing "health and wealth." They preached an ugly gospel of "prosperity." It was Christianity perverted into a glitzy, materialistic, self-centered Christianity. The world (who were supposed to be being evangelized) looked on with horror at the Bakkers' multi-million dollar homes, gold toilet bowl fixtures, and air-conditioned dog house. It was as if Chuck Barris, creator of *The Gong Show*, had become a television evangelist.

Yet, despite the fact that the Bakkers made a travesty of biblical promises concerning "prosperity" and "success," the lesson to be learned is *not* that God is against prosperity and success for His children. What should be learned is the danger of not being accountable to mature men and women of the "faith" in the Body of Christ. The Jim and Tammy Bakker story is the story of a modern day Adam and Eve in the Garden of Eden. They were seduced by evil, and they fell. We should not misconstrue the facts and think that God did not want Paradise for His people. The problem was they were not responsible or spiritually mature enough to handle it.

When Moses led the children of Israel to freedom, they rebelled and danced before a golden calf in a drunken orgy. The freedom God had planned for them was a blessing. Just because the children of Israel abused God's gift does not mean that freedom is wrong. The same is true concerning prosperity, positive confession, healing, and every other principle of "faith."

Fred Price sums this up nicely:

> Faith is taking God at His Word and acting on it. Believing is one half of the coin; faith is the other half. Both halves must be intact in order for the coin to be spendable. You can believe, and everything you believe can be true, but it will never affect you personally until you act on it.
>
> For instance, I have a car. I believe I can get in the car, start it up, and drive home. That is true, but I won't drive home until I *actually* get in the car, start it up, and drive it home. That's the faith part. Acting on what I believe.
>
> For the child of God, I believe what God says, so I have to act on God's Word. This principle to me is the foundational principle for the whole Kingdom of God and everything in it. From that premise, everything else works.[5]

The Tragedy Of Unbelief

When Jesus Christ visited His hometown of Nazareth, he taught in the synagogue. But none of the people believed His wisdom, and they questioned His miracles: "And He could do no miracle there except that He laid His hands on a few sick people and healed them. And He wondered at their unbelief" (Mark 6:5-6).

The unbelief that the Lord encountered in Nazareth is the same unbelief many Christians hold concerning present-day miracles. I think Jesus Christ would look upon much of the church today and throughout the ages and "wonder" at our unbelief. Christians in this generation have allowed a humanistic, scientific, materialistic mind-set to convince them that miracles are impossible. The tragedy is that while much of the church says "miracles are not for today," spiritually hungry people are coming out of the counter-culture and looking to the East, where *NAM* teachers, gurus, and mystics, who believe in the supernatural, are providing answers.

With all this rising criticism regarding faith, people are forgetting an important principle. In one of His parables, Jesus warned about the danger of hiding talents in the ground. In this story, a man distributes talents to his slaves. He gave five talents to the first slave, two to the second, and one to the third—each according to his ability. The faithful slaves who received more than one talent invested the talents and caused them to multiply. When their master came back, they showed him a return.

The unfaithful slave buried his talent in the ground. Because he was afraid he might do the wrong thing, he did nothing. The master severely rebuked this unfaithful slave for hiding the talent, took it from him, and gave it to the slave who had the ten talents.

This parable could easily be talking about spiritual gifts and resources. Do you think God would rather have Christians who are so concerned about doing the "right thing" that they do nothing? Or would God rather have Christians who dare to believe Him for miracles and occasionally make mistakes? The New Testament clearly indicates that the Lord would rather have us move out in faith and make mistakes than do nothing. *God wants us to do something*. My question to the critics of the faith movement is, "What is the Lord's perspective?"

CHAPTER SEVEN

Heroes Of The Faith

In Dave Hunt and T.A. McMahon's book, *The Seduction of Christianity,* the authors state that Dr. Paul Yonggi Cho, Kenneth Hagin, and Kenneth Copeland have been influenced by the New Age Movement. Commenting on Dr. Cho's "visualization" and "dreaming" teachings, the authors state,

> Such teaching has confused sincere Christians into imagining that "faith" is a force that makes things happen because they believe. Thus faith is not placed in God but is a power directed at God, which forces Him to do for us what we have believed He will do.[1]

Later on in the book, Hunt and McMahon say, "Cho's conclusions are in perfect agreement with occult tradition."[2] Although, I respect some of the scholarship of the authors and share their concern over the dangers of the *NAM*, I do not agree with their assessment of these "faith teachers." On the contrary, I believe that Dr. Cho and the others are heroes of the faith and have championed authentic New Testament Christianity. Furthermore, the fruit of their combined ministries—bringing people into a saving knowledge of Jesus Christ, equipping the saints, building a biblical faith in men and woman around the world, and countless miracles of healing and deliverance—speaks for itself.

As a former New Ager, I can say that what these men teach and what the *NAM* teaches are as different as night and day. Having participated in services with all these men, I have observed the powerful reality of the miraculous ministry of the Holy Spirit and an authentic New Testament experience. Joy, power, and the wonder of the Holy Spirit flow like a mighty river of life from these men and their ministries.

Some of the most wondrous and memorable experiences in my life have taken place when I have had the privilege of worshiping and exalting Jesus Christ at an International Convention of the Full Gospel Business Men's Fellowship, the Church On The Way, a Kenneth Copeland meeting, a Kenneth Hagin rally, or a Paul Yonggi Cho service. In each of these meetings the glory of the Lord swept us into the presence of the Father as we sang praises and magnified the name of Jesus Christ.

What Is God's Goal?

Dr. Paul Yonggi Cho is pastor of the world's largest Bible-believing church in the world—the Full Gospel Central Church in Seoul, Korea, with over 500,000 members. At a church-growth conference at Cho's church, Oral Roberts was introduced as Cho's "spiritual father." Dr. Cho's powerful teachings on faith and miracles have influenced people around the world.

One of Dr. Cho's burdens is the nation of Japan, which has a Christian population of less than 1 percent—200,000 people out of a population of 120 million. He has a goal of converting 10 million Japanese people to Christianity.

Oral Roberts said at the conference, "The door to Asia that was closed to the apostle Paul is now open." Speaking specifically of Paul Yonggi Cho, Roberts urged the listeners to "call down the powers of heaven and turn the devil on his heel."

It is quite obvious that Dr. Cho has never been even remotely influenced by the *NAM*. The exact opposite is true: Dr. Cho's ministry is the antidote or cure for the spread of the New Age disease. In the *Christianity Today* article which talked about the conference, the writer said,

> Signs and wonders, usually in the form of heal- ings, are an expected prerequisite to revival and therefore crucial to the Pentecostal "game plan" for Asia. Not surprisingly, then, miracles were presented as an everyday possibility for those baptized in the Spirit and confident of his good- ness and power.[3]

Kenneth Hagin is founder of the Rhema Bible Institute, which has trained and sent out Christian ministers all over the world. He has also been a spiritual father to men like Kenneth Copeland and Fred Price, who have reached mil- lions for Jesus Christ and caused faith to rise in the hearts of many. Each one of these men has had a tremendous impact upon our world by helping people develop super- natural faith in Jesus Christ and the promises of God's Word. Each also maintains the correct balance and priority in their teaching in regard to salvation.

In Yonggi Cho's book, *The Fourth Dimension*, he talks about "God's Uppermost Goal."

> The healing of the physical body is not the Spirit's ultimate goal. You must know where the

priority lies. His ultimate goal is in the healing of
souls. When God deals with you, He always deals
with you through the healing of your soul. If your
soul is not right with God, no amount of prayer,
shouting or jumping will bring the rhema of healing to you. You must first get right with the Lord.
Confess your sins, apply the blood of Jesus Christ,
be saved and receive eternal life.[4]

I think these words from Cho reflect accurately the heart-
beat of his ministry. To suggest anything different is to
disregard the facts. In Kenneth Hagin's book, *New Thresholds
of Faith*, he writes,

God works through us by His Word through our
lips. Jesus said, ''Go ye into all the world, and
preach the gospel to every creature.'' That is the
way God works through us. We carry the Word
to the lost. If we do not carry the Word to the
world then we waste our time praying for God to
do something. In other words, it would be use-
less to pray for someone who is lost if we do not
carry the Gospel of salvation to him.[5]

Here we see Kenneth Hagin preaching the gospel of
salvation as the cornerstone of his ministry. Kenneth
Copeland echoes these teachings. In his book, *The Laws of
Prosperity*, Copeland writes,

To prosper spiritually you must be born-again.
When you accept Jesus as your Saviour and make
Him the Lord of your life, your spirit is reborn and
brought into fellowship with your Father, the

Almighty God. This then puts you in the position
to receive from Him all the things promised in His
Word.[6]

When I tried to purchase *The Laws of Prosperity* and
another book, *God's Will Is Prosperity* by Gloria Copeland,
they had both been dropped by the owner of the Christian
bookstore. This occurred a number of years ago in a city
that was in desperate need of revival. I will never understand what this bookstore owner found so dangerous about
a book that tells people God wants to prosper His children.

Relating To People

Preaching the true gospel of Jesus Christ must involve
relating to people in terms they can understand. Part of
the reason *NAM* teachings like TM, Silva Mind Control,
meditation, EST, and Lifespring have been so effective in
penetrating our culture is because they speak to people on
tangible levels.

Jesus Christ spoke to the people of His day in parables
that they could immediately understand. Today, the gospel
will spread like wildfire if we begin proclaiming the "gospel of the kingdom" that Jesus Christ talked about. We have
done the same thing to the gospel that the church did prior
to the Reformation: We have separated the Bible from the
people by making it inaccessible and "religious." We have
even covered God's Word in a black leather-bound cover and
made it look more like a book of death from a funeral
parlor than a book of life.

Someday we are going to have to stand before God's
throne and explain why the teenage girl had three abortions,
the alcoholic stayed drunk, and the businessman deserted
his family. We must reach out to people with the love of

Jesus Christ *in a manner they can understand*. Do you think men and women today are going to look for answers in a book written in an archaic language when MTV, television, compact discs, and motion pictures thunder a different answer in their own terms?

When Jesus Christ talks about salvation, He is not expounding some esoteric "evangelical" idea about a soul being saved. The Lord died, broke the power of sin and death, and rose from the grave so His eternal life could flood into the life of that teenage girl considering an abortion and deliver the alcoholic from his addiction. Jesus Christ endured the cross and conquered death so His healing power could transform that businessman's marriage and undo a life of misery and pain for his wife and children.

The correct translation of the word "salvation" is "the *total salvation*" of a person's life. It comes from the Greek word *soteria* and means "rescue, deliverance, health, and salvation." If anyone has been faithful to teach these principles, it has been the "faith teachers."

With Signs Following

Although Cho, Hagin, and Copeland all teach the Bible doctrines of healing, prosperity, and blessing, each has his priorities right and emphasizes the most important Bible doctrine of all—salvation through faith in Jesus Christ. All these men, however, stress the other doctrines Jesus Christ emphasized:

> And He said to them, "Go into all the world and preach the gospel to all creation. He who has believed and has been baptized shall be saved; but he who has disbelieved shall be condemned. And these signs will accompany those who have

> believed: in My name they will cast out demons,
> they will speak with new tongues; they will pick
> up serpents, and if they drink any deadly poison,
> it shall not hurt them; they will lay hands on the
> sick, and they will recover."
>
> So then, when the Lord Jesus had spoken to
> them, He was received up into heaven, and sat
> down at the right hand of God. And they went
> out and preached everywhere, while the Lord
> worked with them, and confirmed the word by
> the signs that followed—Mark 15:15-20.

Notice that verse 20 says that the disciples' ministry would be confirmed with "signs following." According to the New Testament, this is how the preaching of the gospel is validated. Before accepting Jesus Christ as Lord and Savior, I observed Christians in action but failed to see "signs" or miracles of healing such as those demonstrated by the New Testament church. I believed that if the Christian message were true then Christians should have been doing the same thing the early church was doing. At the time, I was unaware of the scripture that says, "Jesus Christ is the same yesterday and today, yes and forever" (Hebrews 13:8). As an unbeliever, I was looking for "confirmation" of the word with "signs."

Please do not misconstrue what I am saying. I believe that the written Word of God is the final authority concerning all revelation. In addition, if a miracle or sign *contrary* to the Word of God were to occur, then I would not accept it as from God. Neither should you.

As someone previously in the *NAM*, I experienced many kinds of supernatural experiences. The mere presence of a supernatural phenomenon does *not* prove that the event is from God. We must judge everything—every spirit and revelation—by the Word of God as written in the Old and New Testament. They must agree with the totality of the Scriptures.

> But even though we, or an angel from heaven, should preach to you a gospel contrary to that which we have preached to you, let him be accursed. As we have said before, so I say again now, if any man is preaching to you a gospel contrary to that which you have received, let him be accursed—Galatians 1:8-9.

If a miracle or sign occurs that *is* in accordance with the Word of God and does not contradict the Scriptures in any way, however, then we should accept it as a confirmation from God.

Similarly, all so-called "revelations" must be judged by the Word of God. A number of years ago, a Christian church in a northwestern coastal state reported a number of angelic visitations. The minister gave accounts of an angel visiting them and having a snowball fight!

Clearly, this kind of account should be cause for concern. The evangelists involved in this episode were admonished by a number of Christian leaders, including Pat Robertson. A belief in the supernatural should not be an occasion to throw our rational minds out the window.

Distortions Of The Word

New Age mentors often take biblical principles (sometimes consciously and sometimes just because they work) and teach them in conjunction with their philosophies of life. This is not surprising. Since the time of Christ, spiritually immature and ignorant men have distorted the truth of

God's Word and attempted to make it say what it did not say. This is why it is vital for people to read the Bible for themselves instead of relying upon men to interpret it for them.

Many basic principles of success will work in life no matter who applies them. For example, eating nutritious food is good for you. If someone in the *NAM* eats nutritious food, that doesn't mean eating healthy food is a New Age teaching or that maintaining a healthy diet is wrong because they do this. The same goes for "positive confession" and "positive thinking." People who think right and talk right are going to be more successful than those who do not. Again, Jesus Christ told us that we are to judge a minister by his or her fruit: "Either make the tree good, and its fruit good; or make the tree rotten and its fruit rotten; for the tree is known by its fruit" (Matthew 12:30).

Within the biblical framework, nothing is wrong with "positive confession," "visualization," or "positive thinking." These are not New Age principles. They become sinful only when conducted out from under the Lordship of Jesus Christ. For example, visualization practiced out from under the authority of God's Word becomes "white magic" or Christian science. It is important to grasp the difference between God-led visualization and these satanic forms. Just because the *NAM* twists and perverts something does not mean it is evil in and of itself.

Let's demystify the word "visualization." Practically everyone employs visualization in the normal course of their lives. The architect sees a building in his mind before he actually designs it; the housewife sees a delicious meal before she prepares it; and the screenwriter envisions a story before it is actually filmed. This is not mysticism or occultism—it is a normal function of the mind. Visualization is part of the creative process of the brain and enables us to accomplish certain goals. Used properly, it can also be an instrument of God's deliverance or healing.

For example, a man raised in a negative environment or by critical parents may develop a poor self-image. He has been conditioned to view himself as less than what he truly is. This is not how God sees him or what the Bible says about him; it is the product of a fallen environment and sin.

In order to undo this damage, such a man must begin to see himself in a positive manner. Since he has been conditioned to perceive himself negatively, this will not be easy. At first he has to imagine or "visualize" himself as a person of value worth being loved. Again, this isn't mysticism; it is understanding how the mind works.

Model Ministries

Numerous ministries allow the power of the Holy Spirit to flow with purity and also acknowledge Scripture as the final authority. For example, the Christian Broadcasting Network, founded by Pat Robertson, manages to balance the supernatural ministry of the Holy Spirit with integrity, wisdom, and intellectual honesty. The Christian Broadcasting Network and CBN University are outstanding examples of godly organizations moving in New Testament spiritual power. They are obedient to Jesus Christ's commandment to be clothed with power from on high and bridge it with intellectual dynamism and a comprehensive knowledge of law, government, science, theology, media, psychology, history, and world affairs.

When Pat Robertson, Tim Robertson, and Ben Kinchlow minister in the power of the Holy Spirit and exercise their spiritual gifts on the "700 Club," they exemplify authentic New Testament Christianity working in contemporary society. Ministry on the "700 Club" should be used as a model for other television ministries. Due to the integrity and fiscal responsibility of the Christian Broadcasting Network, millions of people worldwide are impacted positively for Jesus Christ.

The Church On the Way in Van Nuys, California, is another example of a charismatic ministry operating with a high degree of scriptural integrity. For example, the Church On the Way places an emphasis on praise and worship with hands outstretched. Exercising the gifts of tongues, prophecy, and interpretation are a regular part of the service. Everything is done decently and in order, with never a hint of showmanship. In fact, Jack Hayford and the other pastors do not allow any hysteria or inappropriate emotional outbursts. If someone is new to the church and does not know or understand the scriptural mandate for conducting the service in decency and in order, they are gently admonished.

As a result of the pastors' obedience, worship and praise at the Church On the Way is a wondrous experience. It is like being part of a great heavenly orchestra, with every musician playing his or her instrument in tune and on tempo. What occurs is the gathering of the saints in a magnificent symphony of praise and worship unto the Lord. To worship at the Church On the Way is an experience of beauty and awe as the presence of the Lord fills His people and the very atmosphere of the sanctuary, which is appropriately called the Living Room.

The Trinity Broadcasting Network is another example of an organization that combines the supernatural power of God with a strong emphasis on clear biblical teaching. Paul and Jan Crouch have pioneered new ground in Christian television by providing a forum for different opinions within the Body of Christ. In addition, they demonstrate a wonderful example of non-manipulative fund raising.

Although I have criticized the method in which some television ministries raise money and over-emotionalize their pleas—and specifically those in the charismatic and faith movements—this in no way should be misconstrued as an indictment against Christian television. There are hundreds of excellent Christian television ministries, and the National Religious Broadcasters has done a commendable job in trying to regulate and encourage standards in stewardship. Despite some of its faults, Christian television is absolutely essential for reaching people with the gospel of Jesus Christ who might otherwise never hear it.

We must oppose every effort by the government to restrict or regulate Christian television. The attempt to regulate Christian television is the first step in trying to take it off the air. Whatever problems Christian television may have, the worst they can be accused of is using voluntarily donated money for questionable purposes. But we are talking about a relatively small percentage of a large group.

The question we should be asking is why the United States government is investigating the electronic church but not the pornography industry. The combined assets of the electronic church do not come close to the multi-billion-dollar-a-year pornography industry, which is known to have ties to organized crime.

American citizens should be gravely concerned when the government begins investigating the church instead of drug pushers, pornographers, and organized gangsters. We must be sophisticated enough to understand that the real reason for these investigations has nothing to do with the alleged misuse of money but is an attempt to silence the church from speaking out on moral and political issues. As Earl Paulk warns, we will be in danger of losing our religious freedoms if believers do not rise up in large numbers and demand that the government leave the electronic church alone.

Any critic of Christian television should volunteer to answer the telephones or "prayer lines" of these ministries. Recently, I had the opportunity to volunteer and answer the phones for the Trinity Broadcasting Network's "Praise the Lord" program. It was a real eye opener to sit there as thousands of viewers called in with pressing needs. I talked to people who were addicted to drugs; people who wanted to receive Jesus Christ as their Lord and Savior; people with marriage problems; a girl suffering from mental illness; a woman in tears whose mother was just taken to the hospital in an ambulance; and numerous others. It is easy to have a callous heart toward television evangelists until you help answer their telephones and meet the multitude of hurting people with no where to turn except to call a Christian television ministry.

The Body Of Christ

Charismatic churches, faith-oriented ministries, and Christian broadcasters are not the only ones engaged in legitimate and fruitful ministry. Although I speak of my own spiritual pilgrimage and the need to exercise our supernatural authority in Jesus Christ, I do not wish to convey an attitude of superiority or spiritual one-upmanship to those who do not share this emphasis.

In no way should my plea for miracles and the need to be clothed with power from on high be interpreted as a put-down of anyone else's ministry. With humility, I recognize the validity and importance of many ministries with an evangelical or fundamental emphasis. I have been greatly helped and ministered to by those who do not practice a charismatic form of the Christian faith but nevertheless believe in and practice the Spirit-filled life. The ministries of Billy Graham, the Southern Baptists, L'Abri, Francis and Edith Schaeffer, the Rutherford Institute, Campus Crusade for Christ, Rev. Paul Moore, Hal Lindsey, Dave Hunt, Josh McDowell, Bill Bright, Jerry Falwell, and untold others far too numerous to mention are of equal importance in the Kingdom of God. One of the secrets of Spirit-filled living is learning to work with and love all the different parts of the Body of Christ.

CHAPTER EIGHT

All You Need Is Love

The Beatles hit song "All You Need Is Love" repeated the title phrase over and over again. Most people would agree that love is the most important thing in a person's life. The Bible says that God is love, that God loves the world, and that Christians should love one another and love their fellow man. In his letter to the Corinthians, the apostle Paul had this to say about love:

> If I speak with the tongues of men and angels, but do not have love, I have become a noisy gong or a clanging cymbal. And if I have the gift of prophecy, and know all mysteries and all knowledge; and if I have all faith, so as to remove mountains, but do not have love, I am nothing—1 Corinthians 13:1-2.

When talking about miracles, signs and wonders, faith, and the supernatural power of God, it is essential that we remember what Paul indicated as the most important thing. Sadly to say, however, true Christian love seems to be lacking or missing in many of God's people. Yet of all the qualities of the Christian life, love is the most important. It is more important to know how to love people than to perform miracles.

We live in a culture that knows little about real love.
People all around us are starving for love and desperate to
experience it. The breakdown of the family, sexual perversion, homosexuality, alcoholism, suicide, and the rise of the
cults and the *NAM* are all evidences of the loss of real love
in our world. Often, materialism, sex, and power games are
used to fill the void left by its absence. The majority of
New Age practices offer mystical substitutes for genuine
Christian love.

God Is A Person

The true God of reality is personal and alive; the Bible
says He *is* love. His essence and nature are in direct contrast
to the New Age or Eastern mystical idea of God. They believe
God is an impersonal force, a higher consciousness, or
nothingness. In their view of the universe, God is not
personal or living but a totally depersonalized energy force.
This distinction is important to grasp.

When I was involved in *NAM* practices, I felt apprehen-
sive about reaching the goal of becoming "one with the
universe." The thought of progressing to higher levels of
consciousness where I had to die as a unique, distinct
personality so I would merge into "nothingness" absolutely
terrified me. According to the Eastern view, the uniqueness
of your personality is an illusion. Put in the simplest terms,
in order for you to become "one" with the universe you
must totally disappear. That means, "poof," you are gone
forever and ever!

Very few people involved in Eastern mysticism or the *NAM*
truly understand the ultimate goal of their spiritual belief
system. They try to pretend that "nothingness" does not
mean the total death and destruction of their personality,

but that is precisely what it means. A careful study of Buddha's teachings and the other so-called "enlightened ones" will make this quite clear.

New Age philosophy is in radical opposition to biblical truth, which clearly states that you, as a unique person with a special personality, are so important to God that He died for you. In other words, you, along with your emotions, memories, and all the things that make you uniquely you, are of value to the living God of the universe.

God is a Person with a personality, not just an energy force. He created you and me in His image; therefore, our personality is important and sacred. According to the Bible, when a Christian dies, he or she goes to heaven and lives forever in Paradise. You do not merge into nothingness. In fact, you enjoy a personal relationship with God.

The Word of God talks about Jesus Christ giving a great celebration banquet at your arrival called the "Marriage Supper of the Lamb." (See Revelation 19:9.) It also says the Lord is preparing a beautiful home, or mansion, for you. Heaven is a real world with real people not an abstract energy force or ethereal higher plane where you float around on pink cotton-candy clouds and play golden harps all day.

Hyper-Spiritual Christianity

There is a serious danger in overemphasizing the supernatural and missing the importance of Christian love and the "manishness" of man. In certain circles where the supernatural ministry of Jesus Christ is stressed, people have almost a mystical interpretation of life and man's personality. This is not what the Bible teaches—it is Eastern mysticism wrapped in Christian words.

Jesus Christ was the divine Son of God, but He was also human and had relationships with the people around Him.

I have pointed out the teachings on the supernatural dimension of His life and ministry, but equally important was the "supernaturally natural" element of His relationships with people. Jesus Christ knew how to make friends, talk, listen, joke, and eat dinner with His followers. Warm, alive, and tangible, He took walks with them, fished with them, and cooked them meals.

Practically every film made on the life of Jesus Christ portrays Him as some kind of mystic or "other worldly character" hovering above the ground as he walked. This false concept of spirituality has infiltrated the charismatic and evangelical worlds. Ministers strut around as "God's man of the hour" laying hands on people and "whooping and hollering" as if they just stepped off some mystical cloud.

The Lord did not act like that. He knew how to love people as people and take a special interest in their hopes, fears, and joys. He understood the importance of true fellowship. Jesus Christ would not have crisscrossed the country in a jet proclaiming the power of God to people from the synthetic insulation of a floodlit stage or in front of a television camera. Walking among the people, He took the time to know them. Jesus Christ was not a "super-star" or a "religious celebrity."

Christian Love Means Reaching Out

Biblical Christianity is not one-dimensional but involves the full spectrum of life. Revival not only involves the outpouring of the Spirit on humanity, it involves the outpouring of the Holy Spirit upon the friendships God calls you to establish.

Supernatural Christian love and real ministry involves having a relationship with people. Too many ministers do not know how to have relationships with people. I have met men who can inspire from a pulpit or a stage but cannot talk with or relate to people as a friend. Real ministry is not only what you do when the crowds are watching but also what you do when you are alone with people—just you, God, and the person you are talking to.

I remember with great pain some of the early days of my Christian experience. One particular Bible teacher inspired me at a retreat and taught me great truths about abiding in the Vine and bearing fruit. Through his teaching, I felt built up and tremendously excited. Numerous times, however, we had occasion to be alone, and this man didn't even seem to know my name. He made absolutely no effort to be my friend or even talk with me. I was brokenhearted and couldn't fathom how someone who knew such great truths understood so little about love.

This was not an isolated experience. In my early Christian days, I met numerous "great men of faith" who didn't know how to talk to people even though they seemed to have great anointed prayers. Even today, many times I watch "God's man of the hour" ignore the people around them.

This is not the Christianity Jesus Christ talked about but some kind of mystical Christianity or non-personal love. The New Age Movement and Eastern mysticism is filled with such vague feelings of love.

The living God calls us to love and relate to people as real persons. They are not objects to be evangelized or "souls" to be saved. God wants to reach people *with* souls, not just *as* souls. People have distinct personalities.

When we begin to love people and befriend them as Jesus Christ did, they will run to Christianity and not from it. The world is tired of being used and manipulated. All this talk about the Holy Spirit, miracles, signs and wonders, and faith is meaningless without real love.

Holy Wars And The New Witch Hunt

I almost didn't want to write this section because it has the potential of being controversial. My conscience, however, demands that I say something about the recent "Holy Wars" and what I call the "New Witch Hunt." Like it or not, the entire world has been affected by the recent scandals. In fact, Christians in America and throughout the world have discovered that people around them are asking, "What do you think about Jim Bakker and the PTL Club?"

When millions of people consider the claims of Jesus Christ, their minds are now flooded with television images of Jerry Falwell, Jimmy Swaggart, Oral Roberts, Jim Bakker, Jessica Hahn, and the PTL Club. Due to their tremendous media exposure, these individuals have become powerful symbols representing Jesus Christ. The secular world and the news media have every right to look at the so-called "Holy Wars" and shake their heads in dismay. New Age activists like Shirley MacLaine publicly attack the excesses of the tele-evangelists. On a recent appearance of the Phil Donahue Show, Shirley MacLaine lambasted Jerry Falwell for going down a waterslide.

Why would millions of agnostics, humanists, New Age believers, or those who have simply not made up their mind turn to Christ when they see Christian leaders denouncing each other on national television and hiring celebrity lawyers to defend them?

Jessica Hahn, a former church secretary, has accused one of the world's most prominent television evangelists of drugging and raping her in a hotel room. Now she has appeared on the cover of *Playboy Magazine* and posed semi-nude in an article titled "Jessica Hahn—Born-Again." Her price—approximately $500,000. To the cynical secular world, there is no difference between Joan Collins of *Dynasty* fame suing her ex-lover and the "soap operas" of the Christian culture—except the Christian culture may have even spicier stories.

In addition, some Christians almost seem to delight in and relish theological confrontation. It has become fashionable to accuse people of being involved in New Age mysticism and heresy. After all, it's good for television ratings and book sales.

Without question, we need to call Christian leaders to accountability and judge their teaching in light of Scripture. Leaders and teachers who compromise and adulterate the Word of God with existentialist, New Age, or humanistic ideas must be confronted in love. It is intolerable for a professor of Christianity to teach that abortion and homosexuality are acceptable; to deny the virgin birth of Jesus Christ; or to suggest that there are many ways to God. In these cases, discipline must be administered; and sometimes these men and women must be removed from office.

Can We Love Too Much?

In our society, and especially in the Christian world, there seems to be an extreme carelessness in attacking Christian leaders. Obviously, the "flesh" has been responsible for much of the recent *inquisition*. We must be very careful in making accusations against a brother or sister in the faith. If it is necessary to confront someone, it must always be done in a spirit of love and humility. Christians are too quick to jump on each other and swift to judge people's motives. Practicing true Christian love involves believing the best in someone else.

Oral Roberts said something very profound from his Prayer Tower on national television regarding Jim Bakker. He said that if he were going to make an error regarding Jim Bakker, it would be on the side of forgiving too much and giving too much grace— not on the side of extreme judgmentalism.

That should be the attitude of every Christian. If we are going to make a mistake, let it be to trust too much, forgive too much, and love too much. This does not mean that we compromise Scripture, and I am in no way defending Jim Bakker; but we should give people the benefit of the doubt. The word *grace* means "unmerited or unearned favor." As Christians, we must give unmerited favor toward each other constantly.

We must not allow the secular news media to form our opinions for us. Prominent television ministers, especially, should demonstrate the love of Jesus Christ toward one another. In fact, leading television evangelists should get together on one program, take communion together, and make practical efforts to love each other. If this was conducted in a genuine fashion, a hardened and cynical secular community would be moved. A media-oriented hype-session, however, would bring further criticism. Our strength as Christians is not that we have no problems but that the Holy Spirit shows us a way to overcome them.

Many of my close friends in Jesus Christ do not share my perspective on the Baptism of the Holy Spirit, miracles, or speaking in tongues. Yet we agree on all the doctrines central to the Christian faith. I can respect them as true men and women of God and recognize the validity of their lives and ministries. We in the Christian culture seem to be in a hurry to assume the worst of one another, and this deeply grieves the Holy Spirit.

We need to increase our generosity and love for one another and the world. The Holy Spirit wants to give us big hearts. All we have to do is ask, and He will fill us with His love. In light of current events, can we afford to do anything less?

CHAPTER NINE

Deliverance From New Age Bondage

Christians believe in peace, joy, brotherhood, and love. Followers of the New Age Movement believe in these things, too. Many people simply cannot understand why the *NAM* is so dangerous, and they don't understand what Christians are talking about when they speak of the devil and the antichrist.

The New Age Movement is dangerous because it opens people up to all kinds of spiritual bondage that can affect them for the rest of their lives. Often people become Christians but still have intense bondages because of former activities. A person can't immerse himself or herself in drugs, Eastern mysticism, and the New Age Movement and just walk off scot-free. It is true that when someone accepts Jesus Christ as their Savior, they *are* a new creature: "Therefore if any man is in Christ, he is a new creature; the old things passed away; behold, new things have come" (2 Corinthians 5:17).

Yet in my experience, a great deal of healing and deliverance had to occur. When someone trains his or her mind to be open to the spiritual dimension, it is like tuning a radio to a particular frequency. They become attuned to spiritual forces around them.

Binding The Powers Of Darkness

Even after accepting Jesus Christ, I was very sensitive to occult spiritual activity and vulnerable to the adversary's attacks from this dimension. In fact, if I walked into a room where someone was involved in the occult, meditation, or any kind of New Age practice, I would sense it immediately. I could look at people and tell what they were involved in. I didn't want or desire this "gift," but the spiritual radio I had developed would not turn off. Satan had registered a point of bondage in my personality from which I needed deliverance.

One afternoon Wayne Rogers, who used to drive through Manhattan in a Volkswagen bus with "Jesus Is Coming" painted on the side, was talking with me. I shared some of my experiences with Wayne, and the Lord led him to take me into the sanctuary of a Methodist church to pray. We both knelt by the altar, and he laid his hands on me. Commanding Satan to take his hands off me, Wayne exercised his authority as a believer in Jesus Christ and bound the powers of darkness over me. Although I didn't know it at the time, it was a prayer of deliverance that broke the stronghold the devil had placed in my life. I was set free.

After my deliverance, I began studying scriptures on how Jesus Christ defeated the powers of darkness. Soon I understood our authority over the devil. I learned that my former ignorance of the Word of God had allowed the adversary to send confusion into my life. But today my deliverance is so complete and my belief in God's Word so strong that, although sometimes I am aware of evil forces and have the gift of discerning spirits, I am completely free from the effects of spiritual bondage due to my participation in the *NAM*.

The Armor Of God

Many of the tragedies occurring in the Christian world happen because believers don't wear their spiritual armor or hold up their shield of faith. The enemy takes advantage of this and destroys them with his flaming missiles. Remember, physical events have a spiritual dimension. Lies, business failures, confusion, sickness, depression, accidents, and temptation can originate from hell. If we put on the full armor of God, we are protected from Satan's schemes. A series of helpful verses is found in Ephesians:

> Finally, be strong in the Lord, and in the strength of His might. Put on the full armor of God, that you may be able to stand firm against the schemes of the devil. For our struggle is not against flesh and blood, but against the rulers, against the powers, against the world forces of this darkness, against the spiritual forces of wickedness in the heavenly places.
>
> Therefore, take up the full armor of God, that you may be able to resist in the evil day, and having done everything, to stand firm. Stand firm therefore, having girded your loins with truth, and having put on the breastplate of righteousness, and having shod your feet with the preparation of the gospel of peace; in addition to all, taking up the shield of faith with which you will be able to extinguish all the flaming missiles of the evil one. And take the helmet of salvation, and the sword of the Spirit, which is the Word of God.

> With all prayer and petition pray at all times in
> the Spirit, and with this in view, be on the alert
> with all perseverance and petition for all saints—
> Ephesians 6:10-18.

After studying these scriptures, I no longer went around
naked in my Christian life and instead wore the full spiritual
armor of God. I realized that life is a blood and guts
combat zone—an all-out spiritual war—and, just as in a real
war, people get wounded, killed, and destroyed. We need
God's armor to protect us from the hazards of the spiritual
battle raging all around us.

Reverend Jim Powers, director of the Full Armor Bible
Institute, once shared with me a powerful spiritual principle. Every day he mentally puts on the full armor of God
as if he is getting dressed. He literally puts on the full armor
and says something like, "Lord, I gird my loins with truth.
I put on the breastplate of righteousness. I shod my feet with
the preparation of the gospel of peace. I take up the shield
of faith with which I quench all the fiery darts of the evil
one. And I put on the helmet of salvation and pick up the
sword of the Spirit, which is the Word of God." By going
through this exercise, Jim Powers taught me to prepare myself
as a good soldier in Christ for spiritual conflict and alerted
me to the realities of daily spiritual warfare.

The Power Of Praise

Two other weapons I used in defeating the forces of
spiritual darkness in my life were praising God and appropriating the blood of Jesus Christ over my life and mind.
When waging spiritual warfare, I reminded the enemy that
Jesus Christ defeated him on the cross and humiliated the
powers of darkness. One verse that was of particular help

to me was Colossians 2:15: "When He had disarmed the rulers and authorities, He made a public display of them, having triumphed over them through Him."

After declaring out loud that Satan was defeated by the Lord, I would begin to exalt God. The forces of spiritual darkness cannot stand praises and worship to God. Evil spirits literally shiver and flee when we begin to worship and praise the Lord out loud.

A leader in the Foursquare Church used to say, "I love to massage the devil's backbone with hot fiery coals of praise." As believers in Jesus Christ, this is what we must do when confronting the *NAM* or any other spiritual force. Whenever we sense Satan's presence, or if we need deliverance in our lives, let us come boldly to God in praise and worship. Any song of praise from our heart will do.

If you need deliverance from spiritual bondage, just extend your hands toward heaven and begin worshiping the Lord. Something like this will suffice: "Lord I worship You and magnify Your Holy Name. Glory to Your Name, Lord. I thank you for the victory, Jesus, and praise You for driving all darkness from me."

Worship and praise is *vital* for the church. It is especially important for people just coming out of the occult or the *NAM* to live in an atmosphere highly charged with praise. One of the most important things I have learned from attending Church On The Way in Van Nuys, California, is how to worship and praise the Lord. The congregation knows how to enter into praise and worship. Immediately upon entering the sanctuary, you can sense the joyous presence of Jesus Christ.

Purchasing a cassette player and some tapes of the Old and New Testaments can also be of great help. I used to keep a cassette player with a narration of the Bible going constantly, and I still use this as a powerful tool of healing and spiritual growth. The idea is to saturate your mind with the Word of God:

> And do not be conformed to this world, but be transformed by the renewing of your mind, that you may prove what the will of God is, that which is good and acceptable and perfect—Romans 12:2.

Once you have been delivered from the spiritual bondage of the New Age Movement, the occult, or whatever forms of darkness you were or are involved in, you will be ready to move in the supernatural power of the Holy Spirit and defeat the schemes of the devil. In fact, without the Holy Spirit you will be helpless against the powers of darkness.

In an article in *Christianity Today*, Tim Stafford writes about John Wimber, who is called "The Apostle of 'Power Evangelism.'"

> Wimber . . . emphasizes the Kingdom of God as an invasive force, not only proclaiming the good news of the kingdom, but demonstrating its superior power over Satan's kingdom through healing and exorcisms. . . . Wimber . . . scorns the practice of claiming the Spirit's presence purely by faith. When the Holy Spirit moves in power, he says, you know without a doubt something supernatural has occurred.[1]

In the same article, Tim Stafford also says,

> Don Williams, a Presbyterian pastor who is an active leader in the signs and wonders movement,

describes his ministry to drug addicts and prostitutes during the Jesus Movement, before he had experienced the Spirit's power. ''I was taking people off the street and trying to heal them by having them read the Bible and pray. They were not getting free. They needed the power of the Spirit so they could live what their flesh didn't want them to live.''[2]

As someone who lived a counterculture lifestyle, I know from experience and from observing the lives of numerous others that the power of the Holy Spirit is the all-important factor in transforming lives. I know of many men and women who were involved in drugs, alcohol, homosexuality, the occult, mysticism, sexual promiscuity, and rebellion from God who are now living Christian lives because of the power of the Holy Spirit. Millions of people across America have had their lives dramatically changed by a personal encounter with the power of the Holy Spirit. In the next chapter, we'll focus on the Holy Spirit and discover how He can change our life.

CHAPTER TEN

The Power Of The Spirit

True biblical Christianity is a supernatural relationship with Jesus Christ through the power of the Holy Spirit. It has been said that it is "impossible" to live the Christian life. Certainly, this statement is correct. Perhaps the greatest problem Christians face is attempting to live for Jesus Christ in their own strength. Only when you understand that it is absolutely impossible to live the Christian life in your own strength will you be free to receive God's empowering through the Holy Spirit.

Biblical Christianity is unique because believers please God by faith and rely on God's strength to see them through. In every other religion, followers attempt to perfect themselves in order to please God or work out their own "karma."

And without faith it is impossible to please Him, for he who comes to God must believe that He is, and that He is a rewarder of those who seek Him—Hebrews 11:6.

Then [Abraham] believed in the Lord; and He reckoned it to him as righteousness—Genesis 15:5.

This is the secret of the successful Christian life. Nothing is more tragic than watching Christians vainly struggle to please God, and nothing is sadder than going into a church where believers attempt to live the Christian life in their own strength. This is the difference between true Christianity and humanism, the *NAM*, and all other religions.

Before Jesus ascended to the Father, He left some clear directions:

> And gathering them together, He commanded them not to leave Jerusalem, but to wait for what the Father had promised, "Which," He said, "you heard from Me; for John baptized with water, but you shall be baptized with the Holy Spirit not many days from now."
>
> And so when they had come together, they were asking Him, saying, "Lord, is it at this time You are restoring the kingdom to Israel?" He said to them, "It is not for you to know times or epochs which the Father has fixed by His own authority; but you shall receive power when the Holy Spirit has come upon you; and you shall be My witnesses both in Jerusalem, and in all Judea and Samaria, and even to the remotest part of the earth"—Acts 1:4-8.

If this were written today it might read, "You shall receive power when the Holy Spirit has come upon you; and you shall be My witnesses in Hollywood, New York City, Harlem, Moscow, El Salvador, South Africa, and even to the remotest part of the earth."

Spiritual Spinach

According to Jesus Christ you cannot live the Christian life without the power of the Holy Spirit. In fact, *attempting* to live the Christian life without Him is not real Christianity—it is a counterfeit. The reason so many well-meaning Christians appear so powerless and spiritually bankrupt is because they are attempting to practice New Testament Christianity without New Testament power.

Remember the cartoon "Popeye the Sailorman"? Popeye was a weak "whimp" until he ate his spinach. Brutus, the bully, was always beating up on Popeye and stealing Olive Oil. Without the power of spinach, Popeye did not have the strength to defeat Brutus.

In the same way, Christians are spiritual whimps without the power of the Holy Spirit. Most Christians seem content to sit on the "beach" while the devil kicks sand in their faces and beats the living daylights out of them. If they would "eat the spinach" God has given them—the power of the Holy Spirit—they would have enough strength to kick the bully off the "beach" and enjoy God's creation. The Lord made the "beach" for Christians.

Charles Finney, the great evangelist and revivalist, had this to say about Holy Spirit power in his book, *Power From On High*:

> This power is a great marvel. I have many times seen people unable to endure the word. The most simple and ordinary statements would cut men off from their seats like a sword, would take away their bodily strength, and render them almost as helpless as dead men. Several times it has been true in my experience that I could not raise my voice, or say anything in prayer or exhortation except

in the mildest manner, without wholly overcom-
ing those that were present. This was not because
I was preaching terror to people; but the sweetest
sounds of the gospel would overcome them. This
power seems sometimes to pervade the
atmosphere of the one who is highly charged with
it. . . . Strangers coming into it, and passing
through the place, will be instantly smitten with
the conviction of sin, and in many instances con-
verted to Christ.[1]

Charles Finney also relates another story about the
importance of receiving "overwhelming baptisms" of the
Holy Spirit: "My words seemed to fasten like barbed arrows
in the souls of men. They cut like a sword. They broke the
heart like a hammer." Finney recalls one incident when he
entered a mill and was "endued with power from on high."
All the evangelist did was walk into the mill and look at the
workers, who began to tremble and break into tears. Without his saying a word, revival broke out in the mill because
of the work of the Holy Spirit. Charles Finney certainly
understood the source of his spiritual spinach![2]

The Promise Of The Spirit

Since I was not raised in a Christian home but a secular
humanistic one, I have always had difficulty understanding
why so many devout Christians struggle with the issue of
the Baptism of the Holy Spirit and speaking with other
tongues. From my study of the Bible, it seems clear that the
Lord wants to baptize people with the Holy Spirit. In the
first chapter of Acts, Jesus commands His disciples to wait
in Jerusalem until they had been baptized in the Holy Spirit:

And gathering them together, He commanded them not to leave Jerusalem, but to wait for what the Father had promised, "Which," He said, "you heard from Me; for John baptized with water, but you shall be baptized with the Holy Spirit not many days from now"—Acts 1:4, 5.

When Pastor Carl Valente counseled me at the Lamb's Club in New York, he told me to fast, pray, and read the scriptures concerning the Baptism of the Holy Spirit. As I read the words "but you shall be baptized in the Holy Spirit not many days from now" I knew God was going to baptize me in the Holy Spirit.

I met with Carl at the appointed time, and he looked at me from across the table. "Well, Paul," he said, "do you want Jesus Christ to baptize you in the Holy Spirit?" My response was, "Yes, I want Jesus Christ to baptize me in the Holy Spirit". Then he laid his hands upon my head, and we began worshiping the Lord out loud together.

As we were praising the Lord, Carl asked God to baptize me in the Holy Spirit. All of a sudden the room disappeared, and I was kneeling at the feet of Jesus Christ and kissing His feet in worship and adoration. Tears were flowing from my eyes onto His feet as I bowed in humility before the Lord and Master of the universe. I didn't make a conscious decision to bow before Him— it was my automatic response. I didn't feel like I *had* to fall at His feet or that He wanted me to. I simply could do nothing less.

Jesus Christ was the most beautiful, pure being I had ever encountered. He was God, and I found myself uncontrollably worshiping Him. As I did, I felt the power of His love come upon me and go through me. His response to my worship was to baptize me in His Holy Spirit. As the vision in my spirit began to vanish, I realized I was back in the room with Carl. I came away with a deep knowledge of how much Jesus Christ loved me.

God loved me. Jesus Christ loved me to the very depths of my being. All I can tell you is that it felt good to be loved by God, and it still does. From that moment on a flaming torch was lit within my heart, and I began to have a burning desire to pray and read His Word.

I was still attending the University of Missouri when I received the Baptism of the Holy Spirit. At the time, there was a revival going on. The Jesus Movement was in full swing, and we witnessed a mighty outpouring of the Holy Spirit. All over campus, which was a hotbed for the occult, drugs, sex, and rock 'n' roll, college students were coming to Jesus Christ. People literally wept as the Holy Spirit convicted them of their sins.

Members of the Jesus Movement from California rented a deserted restaurant just off the campus and turned it into a Christian coffee house. I used to go there to listen to Christian music and hear people talk about the Lord. The presence of Jesus Christ so saturated that building under a powerful anointing of the Holy Spirit that I and others literally ran to the basement prayer room.

There amidst dripping pipes and puddles of water, God Almighty poured out the Holy Spirit in gushing torrents. With no theology or religious upbringing to confuse us, we raised our hands toward heaven and worshiped God in song and our heavenly languages for hours at a time. The exhilarating closeness of His divine presence was so powerful, real, and cleansing that no earthly words could describe the glory in our midst. As the presence of Jesus Christ filled the room, salvation, healing, and deliverance would always occur. Night after night we met in the prayer room with an unquenchable burning desire to be where the fire from heaven would fall.

When I began dating my wife Kristina in New York City, I had just finished reading Pat Robertson's book *Shout It From The Housetops*. The book talks about Pat and his wife, Dede, being baptized in the Holy Spirit and starting the Christian Broadcasting Network. This had a profound effect upon my life, for I realized that God was master over television and technology.

One afternoon Kristina and I visited the Rock Church on Manhattan's fashionable East Side. As we walked through the door, we found ourselves in the middle of a powerful Pentecostal worship service. People were speaking in tongues very loudly, singing in the Spirit, and praising God. Kneeling in prayer, Kristina literally felt as if she were transported to heaven. She felt what she thought were arms around her as the power of God came upon her and she was baptized in the Holy Spirit. After the worship was over, she looked up and noticed that nobody's arms were around her.

Spiritual Discernment

Every person and place has a spiritual dimension. Certain geographic locations are charged with a particular spiritual presence. For example, if you walk around Hollywood or Times Square, you can sense an atmosphere of darkness. People flying into Salt Lake City often talk about feeling the presence of a "spirit of Mormonism."

If you have discernment, you can tell just by looking at a person whether they practice meditation or some other activity. What is happening in a person's inner life is reflected in their eyes and on their countenance.

Sometimes you can just look at someone and tell they are a Christian. I recall a story by Rev. Jack Hayford's mother, Delores, who leads an intercessory prayer group at the Church on the Way. Delores was standing in a supermarket check-out line when the person behind her said, "You have been baptized in the Holy Spirit, haven't you?"

Often network newscasters, politicians, and actors playing roles in television and film are selected for positions of power because of a certain look. It is an indictment on the spiritual atmosphere of our country that so few people in the media spotlight have countenances that reflect the work of God in their lives. In fact, politicians, news people, and actors who do acknowledge God are often in for a rough time because they do not have that desirable "humanistic look." In a nation that exalts righteousness, people whose lives reflect the glory of God would be prized as jewels and promoted to the top. But in a nation and mass media that opposes the "Kingdom of God," an unspoken prejudice and persecution exists against Christians and those who live godly lives.

People talk about the McCarthy hearings of the 1950s and the blacklist in Hollywood. Right now, however, a massive unspoken blacklist and censorship against anything promoting our Judeo-Christian heritage far exceeds the excesses of McCarthyism. How many major stars, directors, network news anchormen, studio heads, and newspaper editors are committed, visible Christians?

We need a true Holy Spirit revival that will penetrate the major power centers of our society. This will only happen as we prepare and equip a rising generation to face the challenge before them. This new generation must be trained to do battle in the power of the Holy Spirit against the modern Goliath of secular humanism that struts to and fro across our nation. This new generation must declare, as David did, "How dare you defy the armies of the living God!"

Charles Finney had strong words to say about those who have been entrusted by the Lord to train a new generation.

> A theological seminary that aims mainly at the culture of the intellect, and sends out learned men who lack this endowment of power from on high, is a snare and a stumbling block to the Church. The seminaries should recommend no one to the Churches, however great his intellectual attainments, unless he has this most essential of all attainments. . . . The seminaries should be held as incompetent to educate men for the ministry if it is seen that they send out men as ministers who have not this most essential qualification.[3]

You can tell how much truth is being taught at many Bible schools and seminaries by the general atmosphere that pervades the place and by the look in the students' eyes. After visiting numerous campuses, I am sad to say that I didn't feel any difference between some Christian schools and secular ones. What is being taught when the students look so perplexed, disoriented, and confused? An essential ingredient in education is giving people a clear vision and purpose.

Who Is Responsible?

Some major "evangelical" seminaries allow professors to undermine the authority of the Bible and permit a "spirit of accommodation" in regard to issues such as abortion, homosexuality, and the inerrancy of Scripture. Francis Schaeffer warns about this in his book *The Great Evangelical Disaster*:

> Accommodation, accommodation. How the mind-set of accommodation grows and expands . . . . Where is the clear voice speaking to the crucial issues of the day with distinctively, biblical, Christian answers? With tears we must say it is not there and that a large segment of the evangelical world has become seduced by the world spirit of this present age. . . .
>
> For the evangelical accommodation to the world of our age represents the removal of the last barrier against the breakdown of our culture. And with the final removal of this barrier will come social chaos and the rise of authoritarianism in some form to restore social order.[4]

The complacent, apathetic spirit that dominates much of Christian education was birthed in a theology of liberalism and has nibbled away the truth of the Bible like a diseased cockroach. Far too many seminaries and Christian schools are producing spiritually weak and intellectually bewildered Christians. They come out of these schools uncertain that the Bible is true and with their faith in the authority of God's Word undermined. The devil is going to rip these confused, puny little Christians to shreds.

I do not think the Lord Jesus Christ is at all pleased with this state of affairs. While God looks down from heaven and sees millions perishing in a tidal wave of godless humanism and occult New Age philosophies, those entrusted to equip His army have been undermining the troops. It is the responsibility of mature Bible-believing Christians to

keep watch over the seminaries and keep them accountable. This is no small task, for we are training the future
leaders. The Lord will hold us accountable for what we are
teaching them.

Demonstrating The Power

Each new generation—especially this one—needs to
understand their spiritual authority as well as have practical knowledge of how to be effective in society. We need
young men and women who understand the intricacies of
the political process; who can finance, produce, write, direct,
and distribute feature films and television programs; and
who are trained in the legal and judicial system. We need
Christian doctors, educators, businessmen, missionaries,
newspaper editors, etc. In other words, we must have people who are prepared for every field of endeavor—not
people who have been trained in theory but savvy, sharp,
intelligent Christians.

When Jesus Christ taught His disciples, He did not use
mere words to instruct them. He taught them through His
actions. The Lord did not teach theory, expound theological terms, or speak in "Christianese." Instead, He "preached
the gospel of the kingdom" and brought His message down
to a level people could understand. Jesus Christ took the
gospel to the streets.

If the Lord were alive today, He would walk the streets
of Harlem, East Los Angeles, West Hollywood, and other
urban centers. He would have lunch with sales people,
housewives, children, homosexuals, adulterers, alcoholics,
drug abusers, and people involved in the Eastern religions.
Jesus wouldn't be "uptight" or have a heart attack if
they swore and acted like real people, either. He would
love people right where they were. And I don't believe He

would prance around on his religious "tippee toes" in a
$900.00 suit or with coiffured hair.

Jesus Christ is the Son of God, but He was also fully human
and had a sense of humor. He did not float around flutter-
ing His eyes and speaking with an English accent. By healing the sick and casting out demons, the Lord demonstrated
the ministry of the miraculous before His students. He not
only instilled in them a deep belief in the integrity of God's
Word, but He showed them how to *apply* the supernatural
integrity of the Word in everyday life. Now *that* is a practical education!

On graduation day, the disciples received far more than
a diploma. They received the power of the Holy Spirit. In
other words, the Lord did not release His students until they
completed His course by receiving the power of the Holy
Spirit. Only then were His students permitted to go out and
reach the world for Jesus Christ.

> And when the day of Pentecost had come, they
> were all together in one place. And suddenly there
> came from heaven a noise like a violent, rushing
> wind, and it filled the whole house where they
> were sitting. And there appeared to them tongues
> as of fire distributing themselves, and they rested
> on each one of them. And they were all filled with
> the Holy Spirit and began to speak with other
> tongues, as the Spirit was giving them utterance—
> Acts 2:1-4.

Power From On High

Many times in life we need a little "help from heaven."
All of us can use a "super charging" from the Holy Spirit.
Jesus called it being "clothed with power from on high."

Perhaps your life is gripped by fear and anxiety. Maybe you are addicted to drugs or alcohol. Occult forces may be pressing in all around you, or you may simply feel unable to meet the challenges of life. You may have your "act together," but you may sense a deep need for more of God or a desire to walk closer with Him. All of us need to be baptized in the Holy Spirit and receive a fresh infusion of His mighty power in our lives.

If you haven't done so already, you should ask the Lord to baptize you in the Holy Spirit. You receive the Baptism of the Holy Spirit the same way you received Jesus Christ as your personal Savior—all you have to do is ask Jesus to do it.

Lift your hands toward heaven and begin worshiping and praising the Lord out loud. It might be helpful to get on your knees. Then, as God begins to baptize you in the Holy Spirit, you can begin to speak in tongues, your new heavenly language. This is a simple process, and for many people it is not mystical or emotional.

It is normal to feel awkward as you begin speaking in tongues. Since the language is new to you, you are like a baby learning how to talk. It will probably sound a little strange at first, so your mind may tell you it is nonsense and doesn't make sense. When you speak in tongues, you are not speaking from your mind but from the Holy Spirit inside of you. Your mind does not understand this spiritual language, but your spirit does.

The most important thing to know about being baptized in the Holy Spirit and speaking in tongues is that the Bible tells us to do it. The apostle Paul said, "One who speaks in a tongue edifies himself . . . I thank God, I speak in tongues more than you all" (1 Corinthians 14:4, 18). He also talks about why we do not understand what we are praying when we speak in tongues.

> For one who speaks in a tongue does not speak to men, but to God; for no one understands, but in his spirit he speaks mysteries. . . .
>
> Therefore let one who speaks in a tongue pray that he may interpret. For if I pray in a tongue, my spirit prays, but my mind is unfruitful. What is the outcome then? I shall pray with the spirit and I shall pray with the mind also; I shall sing with the spirit and I shall sing with the mind also—1 Corinthians 14:2, 13-15.

Evangelist Oral Roberts gave the clearest explanation I have ever heard on the subject. He urged believers to pray in tongues and ask God to give them the interpretation of what they had just prayed. In this way, they could enter a kind of dialogue with the Lord. Speaking in tongues is an important spiritual exercise that believers should practice every day. By speaking in tongues we keep the river of life bubbling up from within us and renewing our bodies and minds.

As you begin exercising the gift of tongues on a regular basis, you will begin to feel edified and lifted up. Speaking in tongues is a joyous and exhilarating experience that will help you feel closer to God and enable you to pray more effectively. Once you have been enabled with power from on high, you will move forward to "take action" against the forces of darkness.

CHAPTER ELEVEN

Searching For Paradise

The words to a hit song by Joni Mitchell go, "They paved paradise and put up a parking lot." This is exactly what mankind has done to the earth. God created it as the Garden of Eden, but the human race has turned it into a polluted mess.

I remember driving down to the beautiful Florida Keys at the southern tip of the state. Rolling up to the remote end of this string of tropical islands, where the water is a shining aqua blue and palm trees dot the sandy beaches, I was shocked to find a giant parking lot and a huge fast food restaurant flashing gaudy neon signs. There is no question that mankind has turned Paradise into a "parking lot."

Universal Roots And Desires

Author Alex Haley talked about discovering his ancestors in ancient Africa in his popular book, *Roots*. Every person alive today, however, is descended from Adam and Eve, whom God created and placed in the Garden of Eden. Everyone may not be able to trace their family roots back that far, but the fact is that we all share a common ancestry.

Adam and Eve lived in a perfect environment—the Garden of Eden—and it was an actual Paradise. By understanding what the Garden of Eden was like, and by examining

134 Supernatural Faith In The New Age

what heaven will be like, we can better understand what God has in mind for the human race. In other words, we will see the kind of world God originally intended for us.

I believe that the concept of Paradise is powerfully written into the heart and soul of every man and woman alive today. In fact, I think the urge or "instinct" for Paradise is written into the genetic code and passed on from generation to generation. Man instinctively knows that he was created for something better than what life has become today. This dream of a perfect world, or Utopia, is a prime motivating factor in the push for building a better world on both an individual and a global level.

The American dream is nothing more than a subconscious desire on the part of men and women to return to the Garden of Eden. Even NAM philosophy and Marxism are vain attempts at restoring Paradise to the planet. New Age publications continually refer to ushering in a new world order of peace and harmony on the planet. When members of the NAM gathered in remote places around the world to participate in a Harmonic Convergence and "hummed" in unison, they were attempting to raise the collective consciousness of the human race and move us toward what they believe will be a new Paradise.

Adam and Eve lived in the perfect world we all long for. They were in love, and the beauty of Paradise bloomed all around them. Sickness, poverty, and pollution were unknown to them, and they had no problems in their relationship. In addition, they had an intimate friendship with their Creator.

The Authority Of The Believer

God gave Adam and Eve dominion over this perfect world, and since they ruled with authority, all their needs were met.

Everything was under their control. They had no noisy
neighbors or unpaid bills. Furthermore, they were created
in the very image of God and had many of His attributes.
There is still a divine quality to man, and God has placed
enormous potential in the human race.

I am not suggesting for one minute that man is equal
with God or that deep within ourselves we are God, as
some in the New Age Movement teach. There is only
one true God, before whom we all must bow in humble
recognition. We are the creation, and He is the Creator.
Thus, we must have a correct understanding of who we are
and maintain the proper relationship of acknowledging
Jesus Christ as Lord of all. Despite the fact that we possess
many divine characteristics, God Almighty sits on the
throne of the universe.

But the Bible clearly declares that God has given those
"in Christ Jesus" the legal right to rule this planet. In
other words, we have a divine responsibility to exercise
dominion and authority under the Lordship of Jesus
Christ. Much of Christ's teaching centers around the
subject of dominion. Adam and Eve enjoyed this privilege
and responsibility until they lost their authority through
disobedience.

Judith Matta, author of *The Born-Again Jesus of the
Word-Faith Teaching* writes that some "faith teachers" are
teaching that man is equal to God and that the believer is
to "be in control of their circumstances and lives."[1] Theologian's Farah and Rob Bowman of the Christian Research
Institute in California, classify the faith movement as
"aberrational" and single out Kenneth Copeland as teaching error.[2] According to a *Christianity Today* article titled
"Faith Healers: Moving Toward The Mainstream?" Bowman
"is critical of the unwillingness of some faith teachers to
enter dialogue with other Christians."[3]

In their best-selling book, *The Seduction of Christianity*, Dave Hunt and T. A. McMahon accuse faith teachers—and especially Kenneth Copeland—of teaching equality with God. They go on to say,

> This is at the heart of the Positive Confession movement today, and can be traced back to numerous groups of earlier eras, such as the Manifested Sons of God and Latter Rain movements. It is in the writing of leaders in these earlier movements . . . that we first find the major teachings of Hagin, Copeland, Capps, etc.[4]

I have spent thousands of hours researching what the faith teachers are saying—Copeland, Hagin, Hickey, Price, etc.—and have never seen or heard them teach that man is equal with God. After going to their meetings, watching their television broadcasts, listening to their tapes, and reading their books, however, I do hear them teaching that the believer has been given authority in Jesus Christ. Their critics are quoting them out of context and ignoring the entirety of their teaching. This doesn't mean I agree with all their ideas or that I would present them the way they do. But, I do not hear them teaching equality with God.

In the Book of Genesis, God outlines mankind's dominion over Paradise and the earth:

> Then God said, "Let Us make man in Our image, according to Our likeness; and let them rule [have dominion *KJV*] over the fish of the sea and over the birds of the sky and over the cattle and over all the earth, and over every creeping thing that creeps on the earth."

And God created man in His own image, in the image of God He created him; male and female He created them. And God blessed them; and God said to them, "Be fruitful and multiply, and fill the earth, and subdue it; and rule over the fish of the sea and over the birds of the sky, and over every living thing that moves on the earth"— Genesis 1:26-28.

It is clear that mankind was created in "the image of God." This means that we have many God-like attributes and reflect His image in the same way an earthly father's children reflect his own image or a penny bears the image of Abraham Lincoln. The penny is not Abraham Lincoln; it merely reflects his image. The children are not the same as the father, but they do have some of his qualities and genes. There is no escaping the fact that, since mankind was made in "the image of God," we have some of His qualities.

For example, God has given us the power to create to a limited degree. Creativity is a God-like attribute that animals do not have. Only man has the ability to create. He does not have the ability to create a universe with a spoken word, but he does have an extremely powerful capacity to create good or evil. The invention of the atom bomb demonstrates the power God has given to man for good or evil. It also shows how awful power can be when it is not exercised under the Lordship of Jesus Christ.

Another error can be equally destructive, and that is *denying* the authority and power Jesus Christ has given the believer. There seems to be a "modern Inquisition" by some quarters of the evangelical community against "faith teaching."

Again, it is important to make a distinction between having the *authority of* Jesus Christ and *being* Jesus Christ.

One can adopt two possible errors regarding the authority
God has given Christians. One is to claim equality with God
and attempt to *be* the Lord over their lives; and the other
is to refuse to acknowledge the authority that God has given
them.

The Quest For Power

The New Age Movement is primarily a search for power
and authority over the circumstances in life. People instinctively recognize that they were not created to have life's
circumstances rule over them. As we discussed earlier, God
gave Adam and Eve dominion over the earth. The New Age
Movement is a means of trying to regain that dominion.

The brochure for the Whole Life Expo, a New Age
festival here in Los Angeles, states that workshops are drawn
from the following categories: Science and Technology,
Metaphysics—What Lies Beyond, On the Spiritual Path,
Personal and Planetary Healing, New Models for Success and
Personal Growth, and Relationship. Some of the many
speakers include Terry Cole-Whittaker, author of *How
To Have More In A Have Not World*; Kevin Ryerson, a
channeler and Shirley Maclaine's spiritual guide; Jach
Pursel, the channeler for Lazaris, "a spirit being"; Marcel
Vogel, a senior scientist with IBM for over twenty-seven years
and an authority on crystals; Susan Strasberg, the daughter
of famed acting teacher Lee Strasberg; Harold Bloomfield,
M.D.; Timothy Leary; and Desi Arnaz Jr., who serves as the
national spokesman for Vernon Howard's "Success Without Stress" (he conducts a workshop on "The Mystic Path
To Cosmic Power").

The *NAM* is spreading because it has captured the
public's imagination and presents exciting, supernatural, and
relevant programs with "heavyweight" hosts that include

doctors, actors, scientists, etc. The New Age Movement speaks about affirming life and giving people the power to reach their full human potential. The *NAM* has been successful in gaining adherents in the major power centers of society because it proclaims what appears to be a dynamic, positive, and empowering message.

Meanwhile, many quarters of the Christian community seem to negate life and box people in. We must quit playing "theological tiddly winks." If Christianity is true and the gospel is the answer to mankind's problems, then why have we failed to reach the young people? The problem cannot be a lack of concern about spiritual things, for the evidence proves that there has never been a greater interest.

Contemporary Christianity has made two vital mistakes in regard to preaching the gospel of the Kingdom: First, we have attempted to explain away its existence and short-circuit its power through unbelief. Second, when the power of God has been released, we have trivialized and merchandised it like a meaningless sideshow at a charismatic circus. When we return to preaching the gospel that Jesus Christ told us to preach, there will be such a full unleashing of heaven's power that it will seem as if a tidal wave of the Holy Spirit has crashed across this nation.

The recent shaking in the Christian culture is demonstration of God's preparation. He is going to send the hurricane winds of the Holy Spirit upon the nations with a power, strength, and majesty the world has never seen. The hour of God's purpose is almost upon us, and we are about to be flooded with such a mighty outpouring of the Spirit of God that the earth will be inundated as in the days of Noah. This time, however, it will not be a flood of destruction but a flood of the well springs and rivers of life.

Living Wells

Rev. Jack Hayford talks about how Christians can "part-ner" with the Lord in allowing this to come to pass. We do not live in a fatalistic universe, and our heavenly Father expects us to participate in His program for the earth. In his teaching, Rev. Hayford illuminates Matthew 24:37—"For the coming of the Son of Man will be just like the days of Noah"—and compares it to Genesis 7:11—"In the six hun-dredth year of Noah's life, in the second month, on the seventeenth day of the month, on the same day all the fountains of the great deep burst open, and the floodgates of the sky were opened."

Rev. Hayford uses these and other passages to urge believers to fulfill their responsibility by allowing the Holy Spirit to burst forth from the fountains placed deep in our hearts. He goes on to say that it is our responsibility to "part-ner" with Jesus Christ in bringing a "third wave of revival" upon our planet.* Pastor Hayford advises us that we must allow the Holy Spirit to "dig up" the wells in our own soul and ask God to cleanse us of unforgiveness, unbelief, or any other sin that the light of the Spirit of God points out.

Once cleansed by the blood of Jesus Christ, we are encouraged to pray in our heavenly language and sing songs of praise and worship to the Lord. This will release rivers of living water. When we begin to do this, we have the

---

*In the twentieth century we have experienced two great waves of revival with signs and wonders following. First, the Azusa Street Revival ushered in the Pentecostal movement. The Charismatic movement of the late 1960s and early 1970s is considered the second wave. In this second wave, the church witnessed a renewed emphasis on healing, speaking in tongues, and the authority of the believer. The third wave promises to be the most fruitful of all.

privilege of "partnering with Jesus Christ" in allowing a fresh outpouring of the Holy Spirit in our land. The idea is that God is going to use the life of the Holy Spirit, placed like "deep wells" within His children, to flood the earth with the waters of life.

Our responsibility is to cooperate with the Lord and, as Isaac had to dig up the wells in the Old Testament, we must allow the Holy Spirit to show us those things in our own lives that are preventing the free flow of the Holy Spirit. (See Genesis 26:15.)

As this revival of the Holy Spirit begins to well up from within my life and yours, the people we encounter will be ministered to by the life of Jesus Christ. Once people begin to be touched by the outflow of the Holy Spirit working in our lives, then the reason for the existence for the *NAM* will dissipate.

As we have established, the New Age Movement is nothing more than a counterfeit of genuine Christianity. Once people begin to see the real thing in the lives of Christians who are moving in the flow and life of the Holy Spirit, they will no longer want the counterfeit. And after they begin to understand and operate in their authority as believers, the power they need to control the events in their lives will be met.

Exercising Holy Spirit Power

We are at a turning point in history—a crossroad, if you will. God has given His people the power to affect the future. In this crucial hour, we have the power in Jesus Christ to change the course of events. Partnering with God through prayer, praise, and intercession, we can send incense of the prayers of the saints into the throne room of God and change what is happening on the earth.

The faith movement is just the spiritual forerunner of a new thing God is about to do. For too long the power and truth of the gospel of Jesus Christ has been wrapped in religion. God never intended this. But in His infinite love for mankind, God is raising up an army of believers who can reach people with His love and teach them about the total relevance of His Kingdom to their daily life. Faith teaching and the belief in the supernatural power of God speaks to an important need in the lives of people. True Christianity involves teaching men and women how to exercise the power Jesus Christ has given us. This is what people in the *NAM* are looking for!

The New Age Movement exists only because Christianity has been turned into a religion full of rituals that are irrelevant to the needs of people today. A brief visit to some church services is like stepping back in time a hundred years, with worship, hymns, and liturgies conducted in an old-fashioned style. Even the architecture is archaic. Many of our seminaries and evangelistic programs are geared to reach the culture of the 1950s.

This is why people involved in the *NAM* do not want to have anything to do with Christianity. They take a good look at it and run in the other direction. They do not want a *religion* of boring meetings. The people of the *NAM*— your next door neighbors and mine—are looking for LIFE, and Satan has seduced them like a Pied Piper with New Age philosophy. They are looking for the power to keep their lives together, and the church is not offering that to them.

We have turned the awesome beauty and wonder of a relationship with Jesus Christ into a dead, ugly, and lifeless thing. We have turned the wedding of Jesus Christ and His Church into a funeral service. God forgive us. This is why we need repentance and weeping at the altar—not in the form of some weird self-punishment like that undertaken by Martin Luther prior to the Reformation. True repentance means acknowledging that we have not understood the gospel of Jesus Christ. We must turn away from our old works and allow God to send us a spirit of revival.

> Let the priests, the Lord's ministers, weep between the porch and the altar, and let them say, "Spare Thy people, O Lord, and do not make Thine inheritance a reproach, a byword among the nations. Why should they among the peoples say, 'Where is their God?' "—Joel 2:17.

While the false prophets of the New Age talk in the most futuristic terms about energy, human potential, harmony, planetary consciousness, and the technology of change, we offer them "religion" with the name of Jesus Christ stamped on it. The living God of the universe is well-versed in technology, computers, laser beams, nuclear physics, and the like. But we speak about Him as if He were some scholarly gentlemen from the eighteenth century.

The idea is not to be trendy and wrap the gospel in the "buzz" words of our day. But God wants us to be spiritual leaders who are capable of solving the economic, political, scientific, medical, and technological challenges facing our generation.

Jesus Christ has given His people wisdom, authority, and power over the earth, and we are to exercise it. God is looking for men and women in whom to place His divine Spirit. A new generation of supernatural Christians are beginning to move into Holy Spirit-directed areas of dominion and responsibility.

> Then Pharaoh said to his servants, "Can we find a man like this, in whom is a divine spirit?" So

Pharaoh said to Joseph, "Since God has informed
you of all this, there is no one so discerning and
wise as you are. You shall be over my house, and
according to your command all my people shall
do homage; only in the throne I will be greater
than you." And Pharaoh said to Joseph, "See I have
set you over all the land of Egypt"—Genesis
41:38-41.

What people like Dr. John C. Lilly, Shirley MacLaine,
Carlos Castaneda, Jane Roberts, and others in the *NAM* are
scrambling for is the very thing God promises His children—
authority! Joseph was given a signet ring, fine garments, and
a gold necklace as signs of his authority and power. Joseph
had a divine Spirit in him, who gave him the solutions to
the economic problems of his day.

This is what the *NAM* is all about. People are seeking
mediums and channelers to receive supernatural information about how to solve the problems of life. This is what
Jach Pursel, the channeler who yields himself to the entity
"Lazaris," is attempting to gain. A brochure for the Whole
Life Expo described "Lazaris" as "a non-physical entity
whose immense wisdom, powerful techniques and
unparalleled concern for and understanding of psychological growth have transformed the lives of tens of thousands
of people all over the world."

"Lazaris" is a counterfeit of the divine spirit God places
in His people to give them supernatural wisdom and insight.
People have been flocking to the *NAM* because not enough
of God's people have allowed the Holy Spirit within them
to speak to the problems of our day.

Churches across our nation will be filled to overflowing
when we open ourselves to the spirit of revival that God
is pouring out. The Lord is going to bring a wave of revival

to this land like the world has never seen. When we begin to weep before God, our tears will be like the gushing rain clouds from heaven that will pour forth the promise of His Spirit upon the nations. We do not have to fear the *NAM* or anything else. All we must do is seek the Lord for revival, and the spirit of the enemy will be driven from our land.

Soon New Age worship centers will be emptied as salvation is poured out, bringing people we never dreamed would become Christians into the churches. In that day, the large stadiums of our nation will not be host to rock 'n' roll concerts, which have become mass pagan rites of a lost youth culture. Instead, these stadiums will be filled with new Christians worshiping God in song, dance, and music. The churches will not be big enough to hold all the people. I believe this day is rapidly approaching, but we must be available to the Lord and allow Him to work this miracle through us.

> So rejoice, O sons of Zion, and be glad in the Lord your God; for He has given you the early rain for your vindication. And He has poured down for you the rain, the early and latter rain as before. And the threshing floors will be full of grain, and the vats will overflow with the new wine and oil. "Then I will make up to you for the years that the swarming locust has eaten, the creeping locust, the stripping locust, and the gnawing locust, My great army which I sent among you. And you shall have plenty to eat and be satisfied, and praise the name of the Lord your God, Who has dealt wondrously with you; then My people will never be put to shame"—Joel 2:23-26.

God works through His people—men and women—and we have all we need to fight this spiritual war. My challenge to the church is that all God's people will begin to exercise our God-given authority and push back the darkness of the New Age. We *can* do it. We must!

CHAPTER TWELVE
The Problem Of Reality

(The Christian Subculture)

The Pentecostal and Charismatic movements of this century are without question the greatest outpourings of the Holy Spirit since the first century. Multitudes of people have received Jesus Christ as their Savior, Baptizer, Lord, and King. These great outpourings have resulted in millions who have been empowered to speak in tongues, live holy lives, and walk in a new dimension of power and purity. According to Pentecostal Holiness leader Vinson Synan at the 1987 General Conference On The Holy Spirit and World Evangelism in New Orleans, there are now over 256 million people worldwide who have been baptized in the Holy Spirit.

This fresh wind of the Holy Spirit has cleared the air like a summer rain, and a sweet smell lingers in the land. Millions of lives have been changed for the better: Marriages have been healed; bodies have been restored; people have been delivered from spiritual and psychological bondage; alcoholics and drug addicts have recovered; homosexuals lead normal lives; and social reforms have taken place.

Retreat To The Ghetto

Despite the overwhelming good that has been done, the Pentecostal and Charismatic movements have suffered some dramatic failures. One major weakness is the "problem of reality" and the failure to penetrate effectively the major power centers of our society with the good news of Jesus Christ.

Franky Schaeffer has this to say about reality:

> Either God is the Creator of the whole man, the whole universe, and all of reality and existence, or he is the Creator of none of it. If God is only the Creator of some divided Platonic existence which leads to a tension between the body and the soul, the real world and the spiritual world, if God is only the Creator of some spiritual little experiential "praise-the-Lord" reality, then he is not much of a God. Indeed, he is not I Am at all. If our Christian lives are allowed to become something spiritual and religious as opposed to something real, daily applicable, understandable, beautiful, verifiable, balanced, sensible, and above all united, whole, if indeed our Christianity is allowed to become this waffling spiritual goo that nineteenth-century platonic Christianity became, then Christianity as truth disappears and instead we only have a vague system of vague experiential religious platitudes in its place.[1]

Sadly to say, this has characterized much of the Neo-Pentecostal or Charismatic movement as well as the Evangelical Church. After receiving "power from on high," we have not adequately obeyed Jesus Christ's command: "Go therefore and make disciples of all the nations, baptizing them in the name of the Father and the Son and the Holy Spirit" (Matthew 28:19).

The full-gospel church has not made disciples in the urban centers of our culture. We have failed to reach the television networks, motion picture studios, newspapers, stock exchanges, educational systems, sciences, industries, governments, and other power centers.

Our failure to evangelize our society while we glibly tout figures of 40 million "born-again" Christians reaches out and slaps us in the face every night on the evening news when we see moral scandals and the pervasive lack of integrity shake our nation. Night after night we witness new stories about Wall Street stock fraud, white collar crime, politicians and ministers caught in sexual compromise, etc.

If you want to get a feel for the moral climate of our nation, just walk into any convenience store and watch the activities of our young people during the course of the day. There amidst the open pornography and video games you will see the steady traffic of disillusioned youth sporting "heavy metal" T-shirts, smoking cigarettes, and using drugs.

Much of the modern "Spirit-filled" church has chosen to remove itself from society at large and retreat into its own private subculture with its own language, dress, and customs. Instead of becoming salt and light to a dying culture, we have hidden in what many term a "Christian ghetto" and preach to ourselves. The proof of this is that with all the great boasts of revival, there has been little or no penetration of the society all around us. Statistics on teenage suicide, abortion, drug addiction, alcoholism, divorce, child abuse, and AIDS blatantly contradict any claims that we have reached the world for Jesus Christ. More than at any time in history we need true revival. In his book, *Above and Beyond*, Jack Hayford writes,

> How often I have prayed; God give us a sane, solid and sensible Pentecostal revival. Sane, but not limited by man's intellectual pride; solid, but not immovable by the tide of the Spirit; sensible, but not to the quenching of the genuine moving of the Holy Spirit in its valid operation.[2]

The recent problems with some of the large television ministries have only amplified the problems that were already there. My heart literally aches for the millions of thinking young people who have been alienated from the Kingdom of God by the lack of integrity displayed by some who have cheapened the genuine move of the Holy Spirit and have become "peddlers of the Word of God." To these young people, Christianity is no longer a viable option for them in their search for truth. They have become distanced from the reality of Jesus Christ because of the bizarre and dishonest behavior on Christian television and in some quarters of the Christian subculture.

I have only to think of the hundreds of young people that I have met in Hollywood, either in the business community or the film industry—the future leaders of our world—who have been "turned off" by what they have seen. I have met the "boat people" from Christian and Pentecostal homes who grew up without a sense of reality and honesty and are now attempting to find their way home through psychotherapy or an accepting but thinking form of liberal Christianity. Many have been victimized and abused by the "fundamentalist" and "pentecostal" church and now embrace the philosophy of the *NAM*. None of these people hate Jesus Christ, but they have been driven away by a Christian culture that lacks integrity and the ability to communicate in love.

Consider the movie *Marjoe*, about a young child evangelist—Marjoe Gortner—who was manipulated to perform as an evangelist by his parents. One cannot dismiss the film as an attack on the church. This docudrama exposes the problems of manipulation, unreality, and dishonesty of some on the "faith healing" circuit. Look at the backwash of books and articles written by the ex-wives of major Christian leaders. We must honestly say that there are problems within the church that are hindering revival.

Certainly God forgives, but not everything can be dismissed lightly by glossing over issues with a broad stroke of the hand. They must be dealt with from a biblical perspective. Reality must not be swept under the carpet. The Lord is calling us to maturity.

Jesus Is Alive!

Whatever the problems of the church, we are still the only hope mankind has. We must be open to change and open to the direction of the Holy Spirit. We must confess our sins before Him, confident that He cleanses us by His blood. Justified by faith in Jesus Christ, we must affirm and practice the supernatural power of God to heal, save, and deliver.

It is truly amazing to read the accounts of Jesus Christ's ministry and how He healed every single person who came to Him:

> "You know of Jesus of Nazareth, how God anointed Him with the Holy Spirit and with power,

and how he went about doing good, and healing
all who were oppressed by the devil; for God was
with Him''—Acts 10:38.

But even more remarkable is the fact that Jesus Christ is
alive today in the United States and throughout the world.
He is still going about doing good and healing all who
are oppressed by the devil. The only difference is that
when Jesus Christ was alive in His earthly body, He was
limited to being in one specific geographic location at a
time. Now, through the Holy Spirit, He can minister through
the lives of millions of believers in diverse locations
simultaneously.

> ''Truly, truly, I say to you, he who believes in
> Me, the works that I do shall he do also; and
> greater works than these shall he do; because I go
> to the Father. And whatever you ask in My name,
> that I will do, that the Father may be glorified in
> the Son. If you ask Me anything in My name, I will
> do it''—John 14:12-14.

Jesus Christ was telling His disciples how vital it was for
Him to go so God could send the Holy Spirit. Often people
say, ''If only Jesus Christ were alive today, He would do such
and such.'' This statement misses the point—the miracle of
the Holy Spirit operating in the lives of believers. It was to
our *advantage* that Jesus Christ went away. We didn't lose
something, but we gained everything.

> ''And I will ask the Father, and He will give you
> another Helper, that He may be with you forever;
> that is the Spirit of truth, whom the world

cannot receive, because it does not behold Him or know Him, but you know Him because He abides with you, and will be in you''—John 14:16-17.

This is the marvelous secret of the Christian life: The Holy Spirit lives inside of us. Dare we neglect Him?

CHAPTER THIRTEEN

Holy Spirit Dynamite

The Greek word *dunamis* is translated "power" in the New Testament. Acts 1:8 says, "But you shall receive power when the Holy Spirit has come upon you." *Dunamis* literally means "miraculous power," "strength," "violence," "mighty," and "wonderful work." It is the Greek derivative from which we get the word "dynamite"—one of the world's most powerful explosives. When Jesus told His disciples they would receive Holy Spirit power, He meant an explosive, violent, and wonderful power.

Jesus Christ also said, "With God all things are possible" (Matthew 19:26). The truth of those words must penetrate our spirit and consciousness so we no longer perceive present-day crises through the confining limitations of human reason or religious tradition. We have been endowed with *dunamis*! Through the cleansing fire from heaven, God desires to instill a new dream in the hearts of His people. The Holy Spirit is at work in the hearts of men and women birthing a new global vision for mankind.

In this hour of international peril, world hunger, nuclear apocalypse, political upheaval, and moral decline, it is essential to remember that our heavenly Father is omniscient and has solutions to mankind's most pressing needs. The challenge before us is to learn how to open ourselves to His divine guidance and wisdom. At this very moment, the Lord is speaking to each one of us—individually and collectively.

The Holy Spirit's Laser Beam

Modern man denies the reality of the living God and conspires to disprove His existence through pseudo-scientific theories. For example, Charles Darwin's theory of evolution attempts to prove that mankind's existence is due to a random mixture of chemicals rather than to the direct action of an intelligent Creator. Nevertheless, God is speaking clearly to mankind through nature, history, and an inner voice breathed by the Holy Spirit. In addition, the Lord speaks to men and women through prophets, evangelists, and ordinary Christians imbued with extraordinary power.

In a world crowded with the sounds of rock 'n' roll music, television, radio, cars, and chattering people, God is communicating to us through the laser-beam-like power of His Holy Spirit. Laser technology revolutionized modern communications because a single beam can carry far more information than an ordinary electrical wire.

Too many Christians are connected to God through an electrical wiring system when God is beaming three-dimensional visions and dreams through His Holy Spirit. As we receive this empowering and regenerating force, the Lord can augment our human souls in much the same way a crystal prism explodes a ray of light into a rainbow. The laser beam of the Holy Spirit causes our personalities to burst into the full spectrum of potential He has placed inside each of us. Therefore, as His burning light fills our inner being, God's new vision will dawn in our lives.

Dr. Paul Yonggi Cho writes in his book, *The Fourth Dimension*,

> This is the reason the Holy Spirit comes to cooperate with us—to create, by helping young men to see visions, and old men dream dreams. Through envisioning and dreaming dreams we can kick away the wall of limitations, and can stretch out to the universe. That is the reason God's Word says, "Where there is no vision the people perish." If you have no vision, you are not being creative; and if you stop being creative, then you are going to perish.[1]

The New Testament church shook the very foundations of civilization with the saving message of Jesus Christ. Today, the Holy Spirit is stirring the church and preparing for a *dunamis* explosion in a mighty wave of revival that will once again shake creation. A powerful dream and vision from the Holy Spirit of national and global revival is burning in the hearts of many. Each of us must cast aside any limiting preconceptions of what God can do and allow the Holy Spirit to birth His dream for the world.

Shaking The Status Quo

In America and other Western countries, we had almost allowed ourselves to believe that we owned a monopoly on God's miracles. But just when we began resting in this misconception, the Lord startled us by building the world's largest church in Seoul, South Korea, and causing massive revivals in Africa.

The reason revival has tarried so long in America is that we have restricted the operation of the Holy Spirit with our religious ideas of what Christianity is. We have allowed ourselves to settle into a spiritual status quo that blocks true revival. When the Holy Spirit falls as He did on Azusa Street and during the Jesus Movement, this status quo will be shaken. If there really are 40 million "born-again" Christians in our nation, then they are too comfortable and *need* to be upset.

We must begin to see the arms of God reaching deeper into our society and neighborhoods than ever before. His heart especially reaches out to young people. It is *our* responsibility to partner with Jesus Christ and intercede for a mighty release of the Holy Spirit.

Imagine, if you will, what God is trying to do in this generation. Imagine millions upon millions of young people around the world turning to Jesus Christ for the first time in their lives. Do you realize what would happen if millions of young people currently caught up into materialism, the New Age, sex, pleasure, and escapism suddenly developed a burning desire for Jesus Christ?

If we are honest with ourselves, we often doubt this is possible. We have written off this present generation and believe that the world must continually get worse. It is' this attitude of unbelief that hinders the Holy Spirit. We must renew our minds with the Word of God and imagine young people around the world carrying Bibles, running to prayer meetings, and sharing the things of God with each other.

Imagine it suddenly becoming fashionable in our society for young people to carry Bibles with them in shopping malls and on city streets. Imagine the rock 'n' roll radio stations playing music that glorifies God. Imagine the spiritual climate of our nation radically altered by a violent spiritual revolution taking place in the heavenlies, with the demon powers screaming in pain as the Kingdom of God presses back the forces of hell.

The Keys Of The Kingdom

Jesus said all things are possible to the one who believes. He also said, "I will give you the keys of the kingdom of heaven; and whatever you shall bind on earth shall be bound in heaven, and whatever you shall loose on earth shall be loosed in heaven" (Matthew 16:19).

The Lord gave us the keys of Kingdom authority. We have the power to release the full resources of the Kingdom of heaven here on earth. The United States does not have to grow steadily worse. Demon powers can be cast out of a country as well as an individual. We can stop the forces of hell from destroying our nation and reclaim it for the Kingdom of God. Not only *can* we do this, but it is our *responsibility*.

Many Christians have adopted a Calvinist view of reality, which permits a kind of fatalism to occur. The French theologian John Calvin (1509-1564) preached a doctrine of predestination and emphasized the sovereignty of God, thus minimizing the free will of man. The opposite perspective was taught by James Arminius, a Dutch Protestant (1560-1609) who emphasized free will. Dr. Roy Hicks has an excellent chapter on this subject in his book, *The Keys of the Kingdom*, which will provide insight on the influence that Calvinism and Arminianism have had on contemporary Christian thought. Dr. Hicks writes,

> I have yet to meet a person (though there may be a few) of the Calvinist persuasion who has been involved in the exercising of the gifts of the Spirit and in the ministry to the sick by the laying on of hands, as most Pentecostals are. As soon as one believes he has been delegated

power and authority by God, he is at that point moving away from the teachings of Calvinism.[2]

Although Dr. Hicks warns against the imbalances in the Arminian perspective such as legalism, rigid rules, and making "salvation too contingent on man's will, placing too much value on his works and not enough on his faith," he adds,

> The real key to this balance of authority is found in the finished work of the cross. Jesus, our Lord, defeated Satan, sickness, and disease. He settled the question once and for all. He took authority over this world and delegated it to us. Yet that authority must be exercised within the bounds of God's sovereignty and man's free will. . . . If a human being wants to sin and begins to give himself to it, we cannot bind Satan for him.[3]

God Is Talking To You

Within the context of God's sovereignty, we must use the keys of the Kingdom to influence our nation and world. The Holy Spirit is shining visions and dreams onto the hearts and minds of His people. Just as a motion picture projector fills the screen with the images created by the film director and screenwriter, so God is projecting a complete vision on the screens of our hearts and minds.

Obviously, this is an analogy of the way God speaks to His people. The purpose is not to invent some ritual we must go through to hear God's voice and see His vision. But we are talking about spiritual things to the natural man, and the translation can be a bit awkward. The point is that

God can and is speaking to us clearly, powerfully, and specifically in this time. Dr. Paul Yonggi Cho writes,

> Visions and dreams are the language of the fourth dimension, and the Holy Spirit communicates through them. Only through a vision and dream can you visualize and dream bigger churches. You can visualize a new mission field; you can visualize the increase of your church. Through visualizing and dreaming you can incubate your future and hatch results.[4]

There are some in the Christian culture who have a problem with this kind of language. But they do not understand the language of the fourth dimension; therefore, they abort the dream of the Holy Spirit in their lives and the lives of the church. They are connected to the infinite God of the universe through a spiritual telegraph wire while the Creator is desiring to speak through laser beams, fiber optics, and satellite transmissions in four-dimensional holographic images inside our minds. Too many Christians do not understand the full extent of God's power and the explosive intimacy from which God speaks *in the now*.

Our secular culture and an unbelieving church do not understand that God speaks coherently and rationally today. People often ask me how do I know that Jesus Christ is who He says He is and that He rose from the dead. I tell them I know through the authority of Scripture but also because He talks to me on a daily basis.

I am in contact with God! This puts the illusory nature of my New Age experiences on the level of a man who thought he found a bag full of diamonds on the beach but discovered that all he had was a ground up Coke bottle. I have found a warehouse of sparkling jewels and diamonds brilliant in their magnificence! The gloomy mists of New Age enlightenment are nothing compared to the glory of God. Cosmic consciousness is nothing—a mere handful of sand—compared to the awesome wonder of God, who sits on the throne of the universe.

We need to quit putting God in a box and preaching an archaic gospel. God gave men the knowledge to become technological geniuses, yet we have draped His power and majesty in the rituals of ancient monasteries instead of the immediacy of electronic images. The Lord is more wondrous than the command center of the Starship Enterprise in the movie *Star Trek*, but we talk about Him as if He were a senile, hobbling old man and communicate God's authority as if it came from a medieval painting. Meanwhile, New Age deceivers portray their demon gods as life-bearing and scientific.

Ultimately, both perspectives cannot be true simultaneously. Biblical Christianity and the New Age Movement cannot both be true. Likewise, in Elijah's time both God and Baal could not be true.

Calling Down Fire

In the eighteenth chapter of First Kings, an historic confrontation between a true prophet of God and the occult religion of that day took place. When Elijah was surrounded by 450 "New Age" prophets of Baal, a false god, he did not have a theological discussion with them. Instead, anointed by the power of the Holy Spirit, Elijah challenged their authority with supernatural boldness and devised a test to see whose God was real.

> And Elijah came near to all the people and said, "How long will you hesitate between two

opinions? If the Lord is God, follow Him; but if Baal, follow him." But the people did not answer him a word—1 Kings 18:21.

The people agreed that the test would be by fire and prepared a sacrifice on an altar of wood. Whoever's God sent fire from heaven and consumed the sacrifice was the true God.

Elijah did not debate the New Age of his time or argue with the Shirley MacLaines of his generation. He simply called upon the name of the living God with full power and authority:

> Then the fire of the Lord fell, and consumed the burnt offering and the wood and the stones and the dust, and licked up the water that was in the trench. And when all the people saw it, they fell on their faces; and they said, "The Lord, He is God; the Lord, He is God."
>
> Then Elijah said to them, "Seize the prophets of Baal; do not let one of them escape." So they seized them; and Elijah brought them down to the Brook Kishon, and slew them there—1 Kings 18:38-40.

This is what God is calling us to do in our generation. He wants young prophets anointed with the Holy Spirit to call down fire from heaven and consume the pagan altars of the *NAM*. The Elijahs of God must rise up. Will it be God or Baal on Mount Carmel? The time has come to call down the unlimited power of God and shake this world for Jesus Christ—not tomorrow or next week but right now!

Samson, who had been seduced by the spirit of his age, repented of his sins. In one final act of obedience, he was anointed by God with supernatural strength and destroyed the Philistines. Samson pulled down the columns of their pagan temple and sent it crashing down upon their heads. (See Judges 16.)

God is sending a message to us from heaven to banish the mythologies that hinder revival. We must eradicate from our minds the current moral and spiritual state of things and allow the Holy Spirit to birth a new dream in us. In no way should we be hoping for the destruction of people involved in the New Age Movement. We must love them and pray them out of their deception. But we must also call upon the name of Jesus Christ and release God's supernatural power.

Looking To The Past

In the wake of the counterculture revolution of the 1960s, millions upon millions of lives were dramatically changed. An entire nation moved from the conservatism of the 1950s to a hedonistic, Eastern mystical society. The 1960s witnessed a major socio-political shift with radical changes in the sexual, moral, religious, and political lives of the people. What happened in America and England was exported to the rest of the world through records, film, and television.

The reason for these changes was not merely the merging of political, social, and technological modifications. The counterculture shift of the 1960s was birthed by an invisible spiritual change occurring in the fourth dimension—the spiritual realm. As someone who lived through this period and participated in the anti-war rallies in Washington D.C. and the massive rock festivals, I can tell you that there was an energy in the air fueling these events.

Currently, a nostalgia for the sixties is sweeping through our nation. Television advertisers, fashion designers, and the motion picture directors are all attempting to capitalize on this nostalgia. Some analysts even say that the *NAM* is merely an attempt to relive the 1960s. Historians remark that the depth and scope of the changes were entirely unpredictable and still have an enormous impact on our society today.

The church must grasp the full extent of what can occur when a great spiritual change takes place. The counterculture was a counterfeit "revival" or "reformation" that literally shook society and radically affected every area of life. Just imagine the unlimited power of the Holy Spirit birthing a new Great Awakening and revival far more powerful than the counterculture movement of the 1960s. But instead of driving people into the occult, drugs, and sexual immorality, people will be driven into the Kingdom of God with a desire for morality and righteousness. It can happen. Jesus Christ said, "All things are possible with God." The Lord also promises that if we pray and intercede He will bring revival:

> "[If] My people, who are called by My name will humble themselves and pray, and seek My face and turn from their wicked ways, then will I hear from heaven, will forgive their sin, and will heal their land"—2 Chronicles 7:14.

We must repent of our unbelief and allow the Holy Spirit to sweep across this planet. Remember, the word that Jesus Christ used is *dunamis*—a wondrous, violent, and miraculous explosion. Such a powerful revival would be equivalent to a series of spiritual hydrogen bombs going off across the world— not in a destructive force but in an explosion of God's love. Carried by the winds of the Holy Spirit, truth, healing, deliverance, and salvation would radiate across the earth.

Unfortunately, we have been conditioned to think of violence as always being destructive or negative. But the violence of divine love assaults the powers of darkness and despair, sickness, poverty, and disease. When healing comes, it kills disease. Love consumes hate, and light drives darkness out. True revival will bring the explosive force of divine love upon our society and push hell from its midst.

The New Counterculture

We can experience a new counterculture revolution prior to the year 2000. This time, however, a true alternative to hedonism, materialism, and paganism must be offered. The real counterculture should be based on biblical Christianity and confront the new generation with a burning vision from God. Just as the counterculture prophets of the 1960s provided leadership, Christians must step onto the stage of history and provide leadership and vision to a secular, New Age, and materialistic society. We have an opportunity to invoke the full force of the Kingdom of God upon our land and provide the spiritual leadership for this generation.

Now is the time for true Bible-believing Christians to intrude upon the secular flow of history and make a difference. In the same way He gave Elijah a window of opportunity and Samson one final chance, the Lord has given us this time in which to act. If we miss this moment, our culture and world will slide into a New Age totalitarian dictatorship with a loss of freedom and the total restriction of Christianity.

Before we can move, however, we must be ignited by an explosive vision of the Holy Spirit. This vision should be manifest in everything we put our hands to—art, literature, business, music, etc. So much of contemporary Christian music does not convey real energy and power because it has not been ignited with vision and power by the Holy Spirit. Marketing and merchandising is no substitute for the *dunamis* power of the Holy Spirit.

The secular music of the 1960s was gripping and explosive, capturing the minds and imaginations of an entire generation. Rock groups like the Beatles, Rolling Stones, Jefferson Airplane, Grateful Dead, Doors, Janis Joplin, Led Zepplin, and others exploded with energy and power. Radio stations continue to play their songs over and over because young listeners can sense the energy in their music. This energy has been lost in much of today's music.

During the Jesus Movement, Christian groups like the Second Chapter of Acts, Love Song, Barry McGuire, Larry Norman, etc. conveyed an overwhelming sense of power and purpose. Today, in both the secular arena and Christian culture, we often have over-produced music that lacks the burning energy of the spiritual dimension. Music should lead the armies of God and must convey a new sense of purpose and power.

We must let the Holy Spirit ignite us and become swept along by a mighty wave of revival. Things do not have to stay the way they are. True Holy Spirit revival will permeate every segment of our society. As the Hinduism, mysticism, and psychedelic revolution of the 1960s radically altered music, language, customs, art, literature, relationships, and politics, true revival will also impact all areas of our society and culture. The Wall Street scandals, political turmoil, and mass media will be penetrated by a move of the Spirit of God.

The entire purpose of this book is to rekindle faith in the supernatural power of God and bring a wave of revival to our world. I pray that a new generation ignited by the *dunamis* power of the Holy Spirit will rise to the occasion and partner with Jesus Christ in taking our nation and world by a storm of the Holy Spirit.

Lord, in the name of Jesus Christ, I call down fire from heaven upon this earth to consume the pagan altars of the New Age Movement and the self-deification of man through secular humanism. Let the rains of Your Holy Spirit hit people like a tropical storm, shaking the earth and filling it with the rivers of Your life. Amen!

CHAPTER FOURTEEN
The Curse Is Broken

Poverty is a curse not a blessing. Just take a walk through any of the ghettos of America and you will realize that poverty brings heartache, disillusionment, divorce, alcoholism, drug addiction, crime, sexual promiscuity, and despair. Poverty is one of the results of the Fall. It is not God's will for mankind.

Many of those who criticize biblical teachings on prosperity do so from theological "ivory towers" and do not understand how devastating poverty can be. The most loving thing you can do for the poor besides introduce them to a saving knowledge of Jesus Christ is to show them a way out of their poverty. This involves education, training, counseling, and opportunity. But, according to Kenneth Hagin, it also involves an understanding that "as born-again believers we are redeemed from the curse of the law and heirs to Abraham's blessing and God's promise of prosperity." In his book, *New Thresholds of Faith*, Rev. Hagin writes,

> For many years I did not understand that it is God's will for His people to prosper. I thought, as many do, that poverty is a characteristic of humility—and in order to be humble, one must be poor. I thought that a righteous man could not

be wealthy, and a wealthy man could not be right-
eous. I thought any promise in the Scriptures
regarding financial blessing applied only to the
Jews. I have since learned, through studying God's
Word and applying it in my own life, that God
wants His children to "prosper and be in health,
even as thy soul prospereth" (3 John 2).[1]

Co-Heirs With Christ

Ironically, many of the people saying that the "prosperity
message" is not of God are extremely wealthy or at the very
least lead affluent upper middle-class lives. Poor people
need to hear the message of the gospel regarding prosperity.
They need to be delivered from a poverty and victim
consciousness. In fact, many believers need to be healed from
a poverty and victim mentality regardless of their economic
standing. If the gospel teaches anything, it declares liberty
to the captive and tells us that because of Jesus Christ
we no longer have to be victims of life's circumstances.
We need to see ourselves as "more than conquerors." Scripture tells us that Jesus Christ redeemed us from the curse
of the law.

> Christ redeemed us from the curse of the Law,
> having become a curse for us—for it is written,
> "Cursed is every one who hangs on a tree"—in
> order that in Christ Jesus the blessing of Abraham
> might come to the Gentiles, so that we might
> receive the promise of the Spirit through faith. . . .
> And if you belong to Christ, then you are
> Abraham's offspring, heirs according to promise—
> Galatians 3:13-14,29.

Kenneth Hagin explains that the above scriptures tell us that "Christ has redeemed us from the curse of poverty. He has redeemed us from the curse of sickness. He has redeemed us from the curse of death—spiritual death now and physical death when Jesus comes again."[2]

Poverty is a curse that Jesus Christ destroyed for us. He reversed the curse so that we might inherit a blessing. According to Hagin, "Just as the curse is threefold in nature, so was Abraham's blessing. First, it was a material financial blessing. Second, it was a physical blessing. Third, it was a spiritual blessing."[3] This is why the gospel is called the "good news"—because Jesus Christ set us free.

It's as if we were slaves who were forced to pick cotton for a cruel master, and one day we were told a man paid for our release. We might find it hard to believe at first, but when the truth dawned upon us, we would have cause for a great celebration. Jesus Christ said, "You shall know the truth, and the truth shall make you free." What truth was He talking about? He was talking about all the truth of God's Word—not just part of it.

The Bible says that we are "heirs according to the promise," which means we are going to inherit something—the blessing of Abraham. What is the blessing of Abraham? It was material, financial, physical, and spiritual. This is the good news, and it is a cause for celebration.

Kenneth Hagin adds,

> We are to reign as kings in life. That means to have dominion over our lives. We are to dominate, not be dominated. Circumstances are not to dominate us. We are to dominate circumstances. Poverty is not to rule and reign over us. We are to rule and reign over poverty. Disease and sickness are

not to rule and reign over us. We are to rule and
reign over sickness. We are to reign as kings in life
by Christ Jesus, in whom we have redemption.[4]

This should cause us to get up and dance around the room.
We are "more than conquerors" in Christ Jesus.(See Romans
8:37.) Nothing in life can defeat us, for we have already won
the victory in Jesus Christ.

The Blessings Of Obedience

One of my favorite passages in the Bible talks about the
many blessings of obedience.

"Now it shall be, if you will diligently obey
the Lord your God, being careful to do all His
commandments which I commanded you today,
the Lord your God will set you high above all the
nations of the earth. And all these blessings shall
come upon you and overtake you, if you will obey
the Lord your God.

"Blessed shall you be in the city, and blessed
shall you be in the country.

"Blessed shall be the offspring of your body and
the produce of your ground and the offspring of
your beasts, the increase of your herd and the
young of your flock.

"Blessed shall be your basket and your knead-
ing bowl.

"Blessed shall you be when you come in, and
blessed shall you be when you go out.

"The Lord will cause your enemies who rise up
against you to be defeated before you; they shall

come out against you one way and shall flee before you seven ways.

"The Lord will command the blessing upon you in your barns and in all that you put your hand to, and He will bless you in the land which the Lord your God gives you. . . .

"And the Lord will make you abound in prosperity, in the offspring of your body and in the offspring of your beast and in the produce of your ground, in the land which the Lord swore to your fathers to give you. The Lord will open for you His good storehouse, the heavens, to give rain to your land in its season and to bless all the work of your hand; and you shall lend to many nations, but you shall not borrow"—Deuteronomy 28:1-8, 11-12.

Let's not turn away from what the Bible actually says. In the Book of Revelation, the apostle John writes these words from the island of Patmos. Although he was specifically referring to the words of his prophecy, the commandment applies to the Scriptures in their entirety.

I testify to everyone who hears the words of the prophecy of this book: if anyone adds to them, God shall add to him the plagues which are written in this book; and if anyone takes away from the words of the book of this prophecy, God shall take away from his part from the tree of life and from the holy city, which are written in this book—Revelation 22:18-19.

John warns us that we are not to add to or take away from Scripture. Therefore, in regard to God's blessings—material, physical, and spiritual—we must accept what His Word states. Deuteronomy clearly states that all the blessings listed will "come upon" and "overtake" the believer. We must never remove these promises from the Bible just because they don't fit into our theology. Without prosperity, the gospel of the Lord Jesus Christ cannot be preached around the world. It takes money to run ministries, buy television time, and have the resources to meet people's needs. And it takes the power of the Holy Spirit and the name of Jesus Christ to set people free.

Good King God

God wants His goodness shared with all people. The generous King of the universe is not pleased when we make Him out to be a stingy, curse-inflicting ogre. We must not make the mistake the church made prior to the Reformation and separate the people from the joyous blessings in God's Word. Christianity is not a religion of death but a way of life, and God is the very embodiment of love. He wants a spirit of rejoicing and celebration surrounding the entrance of His Kingdom.

The whole point of the gospel is that God's Kingdom is a new and different order than man is used to. Like Pharaoh in the Old Testament, the "god of this age" is a tyrant. Satan is a dictator and rules the earth through fear. *All* satanic governments are ruled through fear and oppression.

The people of this earth are used to a world system of selfishness. Consider some of the world's pet slogans—"dog eat dog," "the fittest survive," "looking out for number one," etc. This is not God's system! Jesus Christ has ushered in a new system and a new order based on God's principles. God is neither a hard taskmaster nor a tyrant. He loved His creation so much that He died for the people of the world. God did not come to the earth to take but to give.

The ultimate demonstration of the love of God is that Jesus Christ died for us. We need to quit wrapping the light, joy, and wonder of the gospel in the grey burial cloths of religion. Jesus Christ is the conquering King of a new Kingdom. The Kingdom is all about love, life, healing, abundance, dreams coming true, and happiness for mankind. The people of this earth—your neighbors and mine—are suffering under the cruel whip of a taskmaster, the "god of this age" and the ruler of this present world system.

Dear friends, in their heart of hearts people are unhappy. In the depths of their being they are crying out like children. They have been deceived, ripped off, and sold a bill of goods. That is why they are scrambling for material possessions, sex, cocaine, booze—anything to fill the burning emptiness inside. Jesus Christ does not want to add to people's burden of sin. They are shackled with sin and death, and in their more honest moments they know it.

The world system is a "spiritual whore" who promises much but does not satisfy. This "Babylonian" system is coming to an end. Our present day materialistic society does not satisfy. Many have managed to accumulate fame and fortune, but still they are miserable. Strip away the facade of the world's pride, and you will find desperate, lonely people. Elvis Presley, Marilyn Monroe, Jim Morrison, and Rock Hudson are just a few of the more famous people who "made it" and "had it all" but had nothing.

Look beyond the glittering illusion, and you will see drug addiction, alcoholism, betrayal, and a hideous emptiness. The movie *The Wall*, directed by Alan Parker and featuring the rock group Pink Floyd, testifies to the madness of a materialistic system with its pounding lyrics: "All in all . . . all we are is just another brick in the wall."

The sad fact is that most people don't even get to enjoy the passing pleasures of the world's system. They watch it from their television sets while their spiritual emptiness is manipulated by advertising and media industries that offer meaning through consumerism and titillation.

> . . . television is accepted uncritically by millions of viewers. Over 145 million TV sets in the United States are being watched an average of 6.5 hours a day in each house. A child entering kindergarten is subjected to over thirty hours of television per week . . . . We spend the equivalent of nine years of our lives watching TV![5]

This is part of the world system the Bible is talking about—a system that sells death through cigarettes, alcohol, sexual promiscuity, and materialism.

> "Come here and I will show you the judgment of the great harlot who sits on many waters, with whom the kings of the earth committed acts of immorality, and those who dwell on the earth were made drunk with the wine of her immorality." . . . and upon her forehead a name was written, a mystery, "BABYLON THE GREAT, THE MOTHER OF HARLOTS AND OF THE ABOMINATIONS OF THE EARTH"— Revelation 17:1-2,5.

Everyone Is Invited

In contrast, Jesus Christ came to set mankind free. He said, "My yoke is easy, and my burden is light" (Matthew 11:30, *KJV*). Deep within themselves and in the dreams they dream at night, the people of this earth are weeping from the tyranny of the present Satanic world order. This is why they feel they must use drugs and alcohol to kill the pain.

Our society has an unwritten taboo against talking about pain and loneliness at social gatherings. This is part of the world system to keep people isolated, compartmentalized, and alone. This is why people rush to the *NAM* and pay psychiatrists huge sums of money.

I read an article recently that said that actress Julie Andrews kept appointments with a therapist seven days a week for years. Imagine the inner pain she must have experienced. The Lord of the universe wants us to go out to the highways and the byways and invite people to His wedding feast. The gospel of the Kingdom is joyous news and must be shared: "And the master said to the slave, 'Go out to the highways and along the hedges, and compel them to come in, that my house may be filled' " (Luke 14:23).

How do we compel the people of the world to come in? We embrace them in love and tell them something wonderful has happened. We quit fighting among ourselves like the Lilliputians in *Gulliver's Travels* who quarrelled over how to serve an egg. The world doesn't care about our denominations or nit-picky theological opinions. We serve a generous King of the universe who died to embrace the world through *our arms*. Jesus Christ wants us to compel them to come in.

The joy of the Lord is our strength. Let us move forth in praise and exalt the name of Jesus. Let us present to the world the glory, majesty and awesome wonder of His love. Let the world see the glory of God as shackles and shrouds are broken and the brightness of the sun bursts through the clouds. The glory of God will do our fighting for us. We won't have to argue or debate when the glory of the Lord blazes in the world's eyes.

Revival is coming, and the glory of the Lord will burst upon the earth. God is responding to His Word. He is not a man that He should forget. He has heard the repentance and intercession of His people and has honored the fasting and weeping before the altar. The King of the universe has witnessed events like "Washington for Jesus," and He is pleased.

We are going to see revival like the world has never known before. Torrents of living water are about to be poured out as God baptizes the earth in His mighty Holy Spirit. If you look carefully, you can see the clouds about the size of a fist upon the horizon. Even now, rainwater from heaven is filling puddles, which will become trickles, streams, and mighty rivers of life.

There is no need to fear the darkness, for the King of Glory is indeed coming. Just as Noah began building the ark when there wasn't a cloud in sight, now is the time to prepare by faith. A new day is dawning, and as members of the Body of Christ, we must walk arm in arm—Fundamentalists with Charismatics and Evangelicals with Pentecostals—for the glory of the Lord is coming.

CHAPTER FIFTEEN

God's Healing Power

Does God heal the sick today? It is clear that during New Testament times part of Jesus Christ's ministry was to heal the sick. The New Testament is filled with references about Jesus Christ healing people from all kinds of sickness and disease. Not one single reference shows that Jesus Christ refused to heal someone who came to Him in faith.

> And Jesus was going about all the cities and villages, teaching in their synagogues, and proclaiming the gospel of the kingdom, and healing every kind of disease and every kind of sickness—Matthew 9:35.

> And he healed many who were ill with various diseases, and cast out many demons—Mark 1:34.

> For He had healed many, with the result that all those who had afflictions pressed about Him in order to touch Him—Mark 3:10.

> And having summoned His twelve disciples, He gave them authority over unclean spirits to cast them out, and to heal every kind of disease and every kind of sickness—Matthew 10:1.

> "And as you go, preach, saying, 'The kingdom
> of heaven is at hand.' Heal the sick, raise the dead,
> cleanse the lepers, cast out demons; freely you
> received, freely give''—Matthew 10:7-8.

According to these passages, not only did Jesus Christ heal the sick but He also commissioned His disciples to "heal every kind of disease and sickness" exactly like He did. In fact, preaching the "gospel of the kingdom" goes hand in hand with healing.

Evangelist Reinhard Bonnke, who has claimed the continent of Africa for Jesus Christ, is an excellent example of an evangelist preaching the gospel of the Kingdom. In his massive evangelistic meetings, the healing and saving power of God is unleashed. Bonnke says, "The nations of Africa are crying out for the solutions to the problems of poverty, famine and despair and I believe we have the answer—Jesus Christ."[1] Miracles accompany the preaching of the gospel of salvation at his campaigns.

The Bible says that Jesus Christ is the same—"yesterday and today, yes and forever" (Hebrews 13:8). Obviously, if Jesus Christ healed the sick back in New Testament times, then He must also heal the sick today.

The Ministry Of The Church

God did not create men and women to be sick and have disease. Sickness and disease are part of the curse the Lord Jesus Christ redeemed us from. Nevertheless, due to the Fall and the resultant factors of pollution, poor diet, contamination, genetic disorders, accidents, sin, and numerous other biological and chemical factors, sickness and disease have entered our environment. Both modern medicine and the *NAM* recognize this and have made attempts to bring healing to the human race.

Due to the failure of medical science to cure and prevent numerous diseases and bodily malfunctions, many people are turning to the New Age for help. It is no accident that the *NAM* goes hand in hand with health food, diet, and exercise. Healing through diet, exercise, and spiritual techniques is an integral part of New Age practice.

Once again, we see evidence that the reason for the success of the New Age Movement is due to the fact that the Christian church has not adequately preached the true gospel of the Kingdom. While certain segments of the Christian culture debate whether or not God still heals today, the *NAM* has risen to the occasion to meet the needs of sick, unhealthy, and hurting people by promising supernatural healing. Simultaneously, certain quarters of the Christian culture teach that God is trying to teach people something by inflicting sickness upon them.

Healing is the ministry of the church of Jesus Christ. People are turning to the *NAM* for healing only because large segments of the church have refused to extend the healing touch of Jesus Christ and have erroneously taught that healing belongs to another time and place.

As in the areas of miracles and prosperity, it is the faith teachers who have faithfully preached the full gospel. While they cannot guarantee that every person will receive miraculous healing from all their problems, they are moving in the direction of offering the healing power of Jesus Christ and the comfort of the Holy Spirit to those who need it.

A Question Of Balance

At times, I have prayed for myself or other people and not seen dramatic results. But many times I have seen God pour out His grace to strengthen someone in sickness, bless an operation, or miraculously heal them. I cannot tell you why I and others have not always been healed, but I do not believe it was always because of a lack of faith. Sadly to say, I know of great men and women of God who have died or are dying of sickness and disease.

The Bible is quite clear when it says we should "lay hands on the sick" and fully expect them to recover. (See James 5:13-15.) But God also heals through doctors, medicine, and science. Sometimes we pray for people but do not see immediate recovery.

Charles Colson, founder of the Prison Fellowship, raises some extremely valid concerns in his *Christianity Today* article, "My Cancer and the Good Health Gospel." In the article, Mr. Colson describes his bout with a cancerous tumor of low-grade malignancy.

> My suffering provided some fresh insights . . . into the health-and-wealth gospel. If God really delivers his people from all pain and illness, as is so often claimed, why was I so sick? Had my faith become weak? Had I fallen from favor?
>
> No, I had always recognized such teaching as false theology. But after four weeks in a maximum-care unit, I came to see it as something else: a presumptuous stumbling block to real evangelism. . . .[2]

While Mr. Colson may not have exhausted all the possibilities of healing, he does attack head-on the areas where certain faith teachers have stepped beyond the Bible. Critics of the faith movement have full justification in pointing out the arrogance of the people claiming that everyone who isn't healed suffers from a lack of faith or has fallen from God's favor.

In his book, *Ministering to the Brokenhearted*, Kenneth Hagin, Jr. has some strong words to say to those "faith" people who are insensitive to the needs of others and arrogantly proclaim God's promises to hurting people.

> Careless remarks do not help a bereaved family! Insensitive words minister to no one. Such words minister death, not life, and they certainly do not fulfill Jesus' commission to us to heal the brokenhearted![3]

Kenneth Hagin, Jr. also relates the story of his fourteen-year-old son who had a brain tumor. After much prayer, the tumor did not go away, so the boy had to be operated on at the City of Faith Hospital on the campus of Oral Roberts University.

> Instant healing had not manifested, so I had to make a decision. I said to God, "Lord, now I'm going to my second option—to my second line of defense. I don't know what else to do. I'm going to allow the doctors to operate, but Lord, I'm going to put my faith in You for the complete miracle manifestation of Craig's healing."[4]

Kenneth Hagin, Jr.'s father told his son, "No army ever enters battle without having a second line of defense." Biblical Christianity is not Christian Science, "mind over matter," or a mystical New Age practice. The Christian should always pray for God's healing.

Illness and sickness are serious matters. We must be careful not to suggest smugly or imply that a person is sick because they do not have enough "faith" or that they haven't been miraculously healed because they harbor sin or unbelief in their lives. We are not omniscient and do not have full knowledge over every situation. To accuse people of not having faith or being in sin is not only loveless, but it also reveals a great lack of spiritual understanding. While these things *may* be the cause of sickness and disease or prevent healing, the most honest, fruitful thing we can do is pray for everyone to be healed and wait for the Lord to work miraculously.

If you or someone you know is sick and not recovering, ask God to show you why. Open your Bible and dig for the answer. Some possible blocks to healing are sin, disobedience, a lack of faith, and a misunderstanding of the biblical principles of healing.

We must remember, however, that *God* is the healer, and the results are up to Him. This is not to imply that He is a fickle God, healing some but keeping others sick. Even though we do not have all the answers, we must maintain absolute trust in God's goodness, recognize our full responsibility, pray for the sick, and take authority over disease and illness.

Fuller Theological Seminary released a year-long study on "the miraculous," which stated, in part, "We reject any suggestion that believers have a blank check from God that offers them certain healing from sickness and handicaps if only their faith is strong enough."[5]

Although I would agree with this statement, the same study says that there is "reason to doubt that the temporary commission that Jesus gave his disciples in Matthew 10 (to heal the sick, cleanse lepers, cast out demons, and raise the dead) is a permanent mandate for the churches."[6]

I wholeheartedly disagree with this opinion, for therein lies the problem. On one hand we have certain faith teachers telling people they are sick because of unbelief; and, on the other hand, we have people attempting to prove that healing is not for today. Both opinions are extremes that miss the truth. Jesus Christ clearly taught that it is our responsibility to heal the sick in the authority of His name. We cannot presume, however, that a lack of miraculous healing is due to a lack of faith. Otherwise, we step out of biblical Christianity and into Christian Science. Proverbs 11:1 says, "A false balance is an abomination to the Lord." We would be wise to remember this verse when considering the matter of divine healing.

Perhaps the person who best understands this is evangelist Oral Roberts. Believing he was gifted by God to pray for the sick, Roberts held tent meetings across the world to preach salvation and pray for the sick. But Oral Roberts also built the City of Faith Medical Center on the campus of Oral Roberts University in Tulsa, Oklahoma. A giant statue of two hands joined together in prayer stands in front of the medical center to symbolize the merging of medicine and prayer.

According to Charles Farah, theology professor at Oral Roberts University and a critic of the faith movement, "The movement is buying into Oral's contention that prayer and medicine must go together. That's a good sign, because it will save the lives of a lot of babies and adults who will get to the hospital on time."[7] We must acknowledge that there have been serious abuses within the faith movement. Some of the criticism against it is not only justified but needed.

Acts Revisited

In light of the preceding paragraphs, I will relate the following story of a personal miraculous healing. My intention is not to trivialize such an important issue, and I cannot explain why people with far more pressing problems have not been healed.

I developed a trick ankle that constantly gave out while I was jogging or walking. It would swell up and cause me such tremendous pain that I had to limp. Then I compounded the problem through an additional injury to my ankle while driving around Catalina Island in an electric cart.

The Full Gospel Businessmen's Fellowship International World Convention was being held in Anaheim, California. The day before the convention, I was getting money out of an automatic teller machine. It refused to give me my money, and, being a deeply spiritual person, I punched the machine with my fist and stomped off. In the process, however, I wrenched my ankle on the pavement. Of course, my ankle swelled up, forcing me to hobble along with a limp.

After I drove to the convention, I had great difficulty walking through the hotels and meeting rooms. Then I ran into some old friends, Paul Corbett and his wife. Paul was the head of one of the Salt Lake City chapters of the Full Gospel Businessmen. Inviting me up to their hotel room, the Corbetts asked me if they could pray for my ankle. To be polite, I said yes, although I really didn't think anything would happen. I was nervous, thinking I would have to pretend that their prayers had worked so their feelings wouldn't be hurt. That would mean acting like I wasn't in pain and attempting to walk when in reality my ankle would be killing me. I know this sounds ridiculous, but that's what was going through my mind at the time.

Before I knew it, the Corbetts had sat me in a chair, laid hands on me, and started praying. We all began to worship God and speak in tongues with our hands raised. All of a sudden they laid hands on my head and pulled me out of my chair. As I was praising God, a wave of light flashed through my body, and I knew God's healing power had touched me. Paul's wife handed me a Bible, which she had flipped open without knowing what verse she would find. She pointed to Acts 3:7-9 and told me to read these verses out loud, which I did. "And seizing him by the right hand, he raised him up; and immediately his feet and his ankles were strengthened" (Acts 3:7).

As I read the verses out loud, I felt the wave of light touch my ankle, and I began walking around the room. The knot in my ankle had disappeared, and I could walk freely without pain. To my utter amazement and shock, I had received an instantaneous miraculous healing exactly like the lame man in Acts:

> And with a leap, he stood upright and began to walk; and he entered the temple with them, walking and leaping and praising God. And all the people saw him walking and praising God—Acts 3:8-9.

In the same manner, I walked, leapt, and praised God. Then, along with my friends, I entered the temple praising the Lord. In this case, the temple was the main hall of the Anaheim Convention Center, where the annual convention of the Full Gospel Businessmen's Fellowship was taking place.

In no way was my healing mere coincidence or mental hypnosis. I didn't even believe it was going to happen. Statistically, the odds are probably a million to one that my ankle would be strengthened in the exact same manner as outlined in Scripture—unless it was a supernatural miracle. In my heart I have absolutely no doubt that this miracle was from God. When the wave of light entered my body and I confessed the Word out loud, I *knew* God had healed me.

The Great Commission

The Bible clearly instructs believers how to handle sickness and disease. One way is found in the book of James:

> Is anyone among you sick? Let him call for the elders of the church, and let them pray over him, anointing him with oil in the name of the Lord; and the prayer offered in faith will restore the one who is sick, and the Lord will raise him up, and if he has committed sins, they will be forgiven him—James 5:14-15.

To press the point, Jesus Christ showed us exactly what His will is when He commissioned the disciples to minister as He empowered them through the Holy Spirit.

> And He said to them, "Go into all the world and preach the gospel to all creation. He who has believed and has been baptized shall be saved; but he who has disbelieved shall be condemned. And these signs will accompany those who have believed: in My name they will cast out demons, they will speak with new tongues; they will pick up serpents, and if they drink any deadly poison, it shall not hurt them; they will lay hands on the sick, and they will recover." . . .
> And they went out and preached everywhere, while the Lord worked with them, and confirmed the word by signs that followed—Mark 16:15-18, 20.

What were the "signs that followed" the disciples' ministry after Jesus gave them the Great Commission? They were miracles of salvation and supernatural healing. The sick were made well, the dead were resurrected, and the insane were made whole. There is no separation in the Bible between the gospel of salvation and the gospel of healing. It is all one and the same gospel.

With Signs Following

When I lived in Salt Lake City, I attended a church called the Full Armor Bible Institute. The pastor, James Powers, had a gift of healing the sick. In addition, he had a testimony of God's miraculous healing in his own life. While painting a house one day, his metal ladder had accidentally touched a high voltage line. Although he had been severely shocked, God had healed him completely.

One day a friend of our family, Steve, was diagnosed as having cancer. It was especially tragic because he was very young. The following Sunday morning, I asked Reverend Powers if he would come over and pray for Steve. My pastor looked at me and said, "Why don't *you* go over to his house and pray for him." I was terrified of the idea, but Jim Powers encouraged me to exercise my faith in God's Word. Although I had spent hours lying beside my wife's parents' pool listening to Kenneth Hagin tapes on faith and healing, I still felt awkward about praying for someone.

Obedient but unsure, I went with my wife Kristina to the young man's house to pray for him. Although Steve was not a Mormon, he had Mormon relatives. Their elders were scheduled to pray for him later that day. I wanted God to back me up with His power so that when I shared the message of Jesus Christ's salvation it would not merely be "words" like Steve would hear from the Mormon elders. Without knowing it, I was asking God to confirm His Word with signs and wonders as described in Mark 16:20.

As I lay hands upon Steve and began to pray, a boldness from the Holy Spirit came over me. No longer was I simply praying for him—I was taking authority over the cancer and commanding it to leave. In addition, I led the young man in a prayer for salvation. As I prayed, the Holy Spirit filled the room, and I could sense that Steve had been moved by God's power. God's glory was so real that it seemed as if a cloud filled the room. When the Mormon elders finally arrived, they could feel the reality of the authentic Kingdom of God.

A year later I learned that Steve had flown to a hospital on the West Coast for further treatment and had recovered from cancer. His parents called to thank Kristina and me for our prayers.

In this account, God used both hospital treatment and prayer to bring about the healing. Jesus Christ used His supernatural healing power to confirm the preaching of the gospel of salvation. In other words, the miracle separated biblical Christianity from Mormonism.

God is good and will meet the needs of hurting individuals who come to Him. Whatever the need—salvation, health, finances, employment, friends, inner healing—the loving God of the Bible wants to meet that need. This is what is meant by the word "redemption." The gospel of Jesus Christ is not complicated. The personal Lord of the universe communicates the gospel in such a simple way that a child can understand it.

CHAPTER SIXTEEN

Firewalking &
Positive Thinking

Positive thinking is essential for success in life. An important aspect in faith, positive thinking is prerequisite to accomplishing any goal. Anyone who can overcome any obstacle has learned either consciously or instinctively to think positively.

Life or circumstances can be extremely negative in this fallen world. When anchored to the Word of God and the supernatural power of the Holy Spirit, positive thinking can produce a success consciousness instead of a poverty, failure, and victim consciousness. Positive thinking is nothing more than making a conscious decision to perceive life from a place of possibilities.

In our highly competitive world, both individuals and large corporations are seeking resources and tools to solve business and personal problems. Positive thinking and principles of success motivation can enable individuals to reach their goals as well as increase their creative potential. Business leaders like Zig Ziglar have developed Positive Mental Attitude (PMA) principles for enriching people's lives. Once again, just because others have abused PMA principles does not mean that positive thinking is evil in and of itself. On the other hand, this by no means is a blanket endorsement of everything said by PMA teachers.

Bumper Stickers And Bedrock

The New Age Movement has sought to meet people's needs by dressing ancient Babylonian, Hindu, and Buddhist practices in contemporary and technological terms. Christians would do well to learn this lesson—not that we want to "sneak" the gospel to people or need to modernize it to make it more palatable. The message of Jesus Christ and salvation is simple. But we have a mandate from God to preach this message of the Kingdom with supernatural power and in a way people can understand.

The essence of communication is to relay information so that another person can understand it. The Christian culture has hollered and yackety-yacked but has not communicated. Billions of people across the globe would willingly come to Jesus Christ if the true message of the Kingdom was effectively communicated to them. In the United States alone, millions of young people would embrace Christianity if they fully grasped God's goodness for their lives. Wearing "PTL" lapel pins and driving around in cars with fish-sign bumper stickers is a far cry from true communication. What person in his right mind would refuse the message of Jesus Christ if they truly understood it?

It is precisely because the Christian culture has not intelligently communicated the gospel that the *NAM* has been so successful. A recent *Fortune* magazine article reported that business executives from companies like E.F. Hutton, May Company Stores, Lotus Development Corporation, Bell Helicopter, and CF Industries practice Transcendental Meditation (TM) to reduce stress, achieve a well-balanced emotional system, and reach a higher level of consciousness.[1]

Timothy Leary teaches a seminar called "High-Tech Methods For Operating The Human Brain," which offers a methodology for increasing intelligence. Interestingly, Leary made this same promise in the sixties, claiming LSD would increase intelligence and produce consciousness expansion. Another NAM mentor, Jack Schwarz, a pioneer in biofeedback, teaches people the "Dynamics of the Human Energy Systems." Apollo Astronaut Edgar Mitchell has established the *Institute of Noetic Sciences* to explore the relationship between psychic power, the human mind, and technology.

The NAM has been highly successful in "selling" Eastern mysticism to our culture with some rather ridiculous occult practices that lack any rational verification—for example, the use of crystals. Meanwhile, many Christians, who *do* have truth to teach, behave as if they graduated from the "Fred Flintstone School of Evangelism" and use prehistoric means to reach people for Christ. But this is not Bedrock, and the *NAM* is not motivated by a cartoon character; Satan is all too real.

Firewalking—Unlocking Human Potential

A universal problem exists among men and women of all cultures: The failure of people to reach their full human potential due to obstacles, adversity, and negative conditioning. Unlike some in the Christian culture, who seem to suffer from a theological introspection akin to an infected ingrown toe-nail, the NAM moves outward in a satanically-inspired false evangelistic thrust. Offering techniques that apparently help people solve their problems, they promise the means for unlocking human potential.

In their more dramatic forms, NAM teachers like Richard Greene teach courses on "firewalking" and mind expansion. In these courses, students learn how to walk over fiery coals barefoot. Firewalking teaches people that if they can learn to walk over burning coals barefoot using the powers of their mind, they can solve any problem in life. Firewalking is an ancient yogic practice that began in India.

But unlocking human potential, positive thinking, and the power resident in the human mind is *not* the exclusive domain of the New Age Movement. *God* created the human mind and placed enormous resident power within the consciousness of men and women. Modern psychology tells us that the vast majority of people do not even use 10 percent of their mind. If this is true, then 90 percent of the human mind remains unused!

While Christians point fingers and call men sinners, the NAM talks about helping people reach their full potential and has created the "Human Potential Movement." Yes, man *is* sinful and separated from God. Homosexuality, pornography, drugs, abortion, and divorce are wrong, and we must oppose evil in all its forms and fight for what is right. But Jesus Christ did not call us to be the moral policemen of the world. We have been called to bring the life of Jesus Christ to the lost; we must present an alternative.

Christians must show people a new and living way. This is the message of the Kingdom! The awesome, liberating power of Jesus Christ and the glory of God is so exciting and contagious that it will spread unrestrained when the dead orthodoxy of religion is unchained. Within the Lordship of Jesus Christ exists a limitless dimension of human potential and intelligence. As Christ's ambassadors, we must help people explore these frontiers.

Do you understand what revival is? It is allowing the full force of Holy Spirit New Testament power to sweep through the world once again. Let Pentecost come out of the Upper Room and spread out onto the streets. World travelers rave about the brilliant colors of the Aurora Borealis. But we have something far more powerful, awesome, and wonderful than that—the full splendor and majesty of the Holy Spirit rising inside us in rivers of life.

Jesus Christ is commanding the church to "come forth" from its burial tomb of dead religious works. The Lord is commanding His bride to come alive with resurrection power. Can you feel the force of God's mighty power? The same power that spoke the universe into being and breathed life into man at creation is stirring the church. *Now* is the time to allow the full force of God's mighty presence and power to fill the earth. Christians should be the ones teaching firewalking—walking in the revival fire of the Holy Spirit!

God is the Creator of the universe. When it comes to evangelism, we must allow Him to ignite our minds with the lightning flashes of His imagination. We must stop serving the gospel as "warmed over corned-beef hash" when Jesus Christ has told us to *compel* people to come to a magnificent, delicious feast.

Our Lord is not represented in the mystical paintings of Salvador Dali or the overly religious paintings of the Middle Ages. God has given us a "technicolor raincoat" and placed a ring on our fingers. He has prepared the fatted calf for the Prodigal Son (our present generation). As the prodigal son discovered that living with the pigs was no fun, so eventually those in the NAM will discover its bankruptcy (as did their spiritual predecessors in the counterculture).

True evangelism means preparing a glorious feast and celebration of the good news of Jesus Christ. The hedonistic "party animals" of this generation will turn from their rebellion when we invite them to God's eternal cosmic party!

Flirting With The New Age

Some so-called Christians *have* deserted the historic Christian faith for NAM teachings wrapped in Christian garb.

Men like the late Bishop Pike and more recently Rodney R. Romney, senior minister of Seattle's First Baptist Church (who wrote *Journey To Inner Space: Finding God-In-Us*), have clearly strayed from orthodox biblical doctrine into error. Religious Science, Unity, Christian Science, and the like are dangerous attempts to mix biblical teaching with Eastern mysticism. These teachings adulterate the Word of God and should be considered apostasy.

Yet there is room for things like positive thinking within the clear biblical framework of the Old and New Testaments as long as it is rooted and grounded in the Bible. Ministers such as Norman Vincent Peale have popularized positive thinking (PMA) through television and books. Rev. Peale's book, *The Power of Positive Thinking,* is perhaps the classic work on the subject. PMA has helped millions of people around the world overcome obstacles and achieve goals. In his book, *The Secret Kingdom*, however, Pat Robertson gives us a word of warning:

> . . . "positive mental attitude," or PMA, is indeed important . . . negative attitudes can vitiate our most valiant attempts. Conversely, positive thinking will more often than not lead to successful action.
>
> Unfortunately, such people as Napoleon Hill, who wrote *Think and Grow Rich*, have gleaned only a few truths of the kingdom of God. They try to gain the kingdom without submitting themselves to the King. . . .
>
> Without the Lordship of Jesus, these benefits are both transitory and harmful. In fact, many advocates of mind over matter ultimately end in hellish spiritism.[2]

Although a book like Napoleon Hill's *Think and Grow Rich* contains a number of true principles for learning how to accumulate wealth, reading such books takes spiritual discernment and a thorough knowledge of the Bible. Napoleon Hill departs from sound biblical doctrine by encouraging the use of what he terms the "Master Mind Principle," which encourages people to use both mental imagination and psychic energy to contact great men of the past like Henry Ford, Ghandi, Thomas Edison, etc. Without question, these practices enter the realm of the occult and are in direct disobedience to the liberating commandments of God.

Other books like *Success Through Positive Mental Attitude* by Napoleon Hill and W. Clement Stone, *Psychocybernetics and Self Fulfillment* by Maxwell Maltz, M.D., and *How To Win Friends And Influence People* by Dale Carnegie do contain success principles that are in the framework of the Bible. But this does not mean that they should be read without discernment.

It is important to understand that not all secular thought is contrary to biblical teachings. A wide body of literature and information on subjects such as success motivation, positive thinking, psychology, literature, business, art, film, etc. exists and can be of great benefit. The key is to evaluate these in light of Scripture.

Some are calling for the church to be the censor of all that is not specifically Christian. This produces a narrow, ugly, and pietistic world of false spirituality. For example, a secular psychotherapist or filmmaker may have something of value to say to the Christian or non-Christian. That does not mean we must accept their world view in its entirety, but we must be spiritually mature enough to recognize the good from the bad.

Finally, the authority of Scripture is our ultimate reference point. Anything that contradicts the clear teaching of the Bible in reference to spirituality, morality, or sexuality must be rejected.

Victim Consciousness And Psychological Pain

Many people alive today suffer from poverty, failure, and victim consciousness. They have been raised in extremely negative childhood environments that often included parents who suffered from poverty consciousness and poor self-esteem. In addition, many people grow up as victims of criticism, emotional abuse, sexual molestation, and alcoholism etc. Modern psychologists from Carl Jung to Carl Rogers—as well as *NAM* teachers—have attempted to address these issues in the lives of hurting people.

A child raised in a negative environment learns subconsciously to develop a victim consciousness. Jesus Christ died to set us free from this mind-set so we could have "fullness of life." Freudian psychology, reality therapy, biofeedback, encounter groups, hypnosis, mood altering drugs, Alcoholics Anonymous, Silva Mind Control, Est, and meditation are all attempts to undo the adverse effects of negative conditioning. Often Christians dismiss these activities as heretical ideas without taking the time to feel the pain and understand the problems of others. People who hurt inside are not going to investigate theology; they are going to grab what works and what is offered to them.

Sometimes people intellectualize or philosophize their pain and suffering. Many people involved in the *NAM*, cults, and radical politics are trying to escape inner psychological pain. I understand this because I experienced a great deal of pain in my own life. Coming from a family with a history of alcoholism, I experienced the fractured and distorted survival mechanisms that often develop in children of alcoholics. Due to the disturbed psychological patterns and emotional havoc created in my personality, these defense mechanisms were my means of coping with life. Much of my involvement in radical politics, drugs, and New Age activities were exemplary of someone in great pain.

While I was taking drugs and organizing demonstrations in high school, my mother took me to a psychological counselor. In therapy, I was encouraged to talk about my deepest feelings. Ultimately, psychotherapy did not give me the power, answers, or healing I was looking for. This came later when I accepted Jesus Christ into my life and began walking in partnership with Him.

Not all of the inner healing in my life has been instantaneous, but Jesus Christ has been faithful to carry my burdens of psychological pain, insecurity, anxiety, fear, and depression. In addition, I have experienced the Holy Spirit as He has moved with great healing power in my personality and in the lives of people for whom I have prayed. I know Jesus Christ as the "great psychiatrist" and have experienced His healing power in the deepest recesses of my personality. I have also learned the marvelous secret of transparency and openness. As I live the life in Jesus Christ as a witness to a watching world, I never have to *act* like a Christian or put on a show of having my "act together."

We will not win the world to Jesus Christ by putting on a bravado of spirituality. We are who we are—good and bad. We must know who we are in our humanity with all our strengths and weaknesses. It is not we who win people to Jesus Christ; it is the Holy Spirit in us. The victorious secret of the Christian life is that Jesus Christ lives inside of us! We are free in our humanness to trust the Holy Spirit to work through us. I am not talking about false humility.

You and I as distinct personalities are important to God. Our uniqueness and individualism are to be expressed not denied.

Richard Alpert, who after his mystical journey to India became the guru "Baba Ram Dass," talks a lot about the "cosmic dance" in his book, *Be Here Now*. When I practiced the teachings of Baba Ram Dass, I was never able to enjoy the dance of life. The only way to attain such peace is in relationship to Jesus Christ. But while I am dancing with Jesus Christ in my heart of hearts, I have experienced enough pain to be sensitive to the hurts of others.

The gospel of Jesus Christ contains the answers to mankind's pain and suffering. If applied, these powerful biblical principles can alleviate human suffering. Kenneth Hagin says, "Many people fail because they see themselves as failing. If they are sick, they think of themselves as dying."[3] By thinking positively in accordance with the clear teaching of the Scriptures, we can learn to see ourselves as the Word of God says we are. This will set us free from the curse of negative childhood experiences.

Letting God Take Control

Nothing is more terrifying or frightening than the desperate feeling of being trapped by inner psychological or spiritual forces beyond our control. This is the appeal of both psychological therapy and the *NAM*. Both promise deliverance and rescuing from the endless treadmill of forces that keep us from being all we were created to be or from seeing our dreams come true. Each person alive has a dream of what they would like to become or what they would like their lives to be.

Often economic, educational, psychological, and spiritual factors lock us out from the blessings God desires for us to have. Marilyn Hickey teaches that negative behavior such as sexual immorality, alcoholism, and poverty is passed on from generation to generation. In this biblical view, negative problems have their origins in spiritual bondage rather than conflicts between the *Id* and *Super Ego,* as Freud suggests. Instead of using psychoanalysis, Marilyn Hickey teaches people to use the "kingdom authority" Jesus Christ gave His followers to "bind the generational curse" over their families and thus free people to be all they were created to be.

Dr. Fred Price, who has established the Crenshaw Christian Center in the middle of an impoverished area of Los Angeles, teaches people that they can be successful in all areas of life through the power of Jesus Christ. According to Dr. Price, "If you don't like the circumstances of your life then change [them]. But before you can change what's going on out here you have to change what's going on in here."[4]

This touches on the central nerve that affects all humanity. For the most part, people feel trapped and imprisoned by a variety of forces beyond their control. The brutality of this feeling can be overwhelming at times and drive people to desperate means to solve their dilemma. As babies cry to elicit their parents' help in meeting their most basic needs, so modern man also "cries" in an attempt to meet what psychologist Abraham Maslow termed "The Hierarchy of Human Needs." Listed in progressive order they are,

1. *Psychological*—the need for food, clothing, and shelter.
2. *Safety*—security from an exterior danger.
3. *Belongingness* and *love.*
4. *Esteem*—personal and outside recognition that one is worthy.

5. *Self-Actualization*.
6. The *desire to know* and *understand*.[5]

With mature people, "crying" often takes more sophisticated forms, but the level of intensity is the same as the young child's. In the depths of their souls, people are crying out for some kind of celestial parent to rescue them. This is not an accident but a deliberate spiritual mechanism placed inside the heart of every man and woman by their loving heavenly Father. Pain and suffering of unmet needs can be the means by which God draws people to Himself—not that pain and suffering are the will of God for people; but the Lord will use it to turn hearts toward heaven.

As long as it is rooted and grounded in clear biblical teaching, positive thinking has a place as a spiritual resource in helping us develop a success consciousness. Positive thinking becomes idolatrous or sinful only when it takes the place of our recognizing our need of a Savior and thwarts our acknowledgement of God's existence at the deepest levels of our personality. It is in intense pain and suffering that we have the privilege and unique joy of turning to God in faith and allowing His hand to rescue and deliver us.

The Danger Of Self-Deification

In the final analysis, positive thinking and faith teaching can be instruments of our appropriating "Kingdom power" in our lives. But they also have the potential for planting seeds of self-deification in the dark places of our fleshly hearts. Supernatural Kingdom authority and a renewed mind are blessings to be enjoyed as our inheritance in Jesus Christ. We must, however, steer clear of the extremely subtle temptation to "be God." This is Satan's great sin, and, as

I mentioned earlier, it was Adam and Eve's temptation "to be like God" that allowed sin to enter the human race. (See Genesis 3.)

The critics of positive thinking and the faith movement are right in pointing out the dangers of self-deification. The spiritual root of all sin, this desire to be God, is at the core of the New Age Movement and the philosophy of secular humanism.

In our heart of hearts we must, by the power of the Holy Spirit, put to death the secret desire of our flesh resident in our fallen nature to be God. Final release, victory, and resurrection occurs when we fully acknowledge Jesus Christ as Lord in the center of our being. It is in this posture of true humility, worship, and adoration that we become all we were created to be. The danger of secular humanist philosophy, the *NAM*, and some "faith teaching" is that it can seduce the pride of man. The full release of human potential cannot be achieved by any self-effort but by laying aside these things and accepting God's salvation in Jesus Christ.

This is only possible when through faith we have absolute assurance and confidence in God's goodness and the fact that, just like a good earthly father, He wants the very best for us. This is what real faith teaching and positive thinking is all about.

CHAPTER SEVENTEEN

Commanding The Mountain To Move

Perhaps the greatest area of debate surrounding the faith movement besides divine healing and prosperity is positive confession. Faith teachers are often called "name-it-and-claim-it-folks." We have found that there have been abuses regarding the biblical principle of confessing God's Word. Some have tried to turn speaking God's Word into a technique for making God a heavenly butler whom they can send scurrying for coffee or salad. Once again, however, it is important that we don't "throw the baby out with the bathwater."

Power Of The Spoken Word

What they say about New Yorkers is true—we are obnoxious, pushy snobs. I was convinced that the United States ended at the Hudson River; except for California, nothing existed between New York and Los Angeles. The first time I listened to a faith teacher, I was deeply offended by the man's mid-western drawl. Then, every cassette tape I heard of a faith teacher had some guy talking in a Texas or Oklahoma accent. Not once did I hear someone with an eastern accent preaching on "positive confession" or faith. To make matters worse, Charles Capps, who gave some profound teaching on confessing God's Word, had an Arkansas drawl!

Yet as soon as I heard their message, I knew these men were on to something and had tapped into the hurricane force of God's power. They kept pounding home a message of supernatural faith in the authority of God's Word. As I listened, something clicked inside of me and told me their message was true. It was humbling for me to admit that these Texas, Oklahoma, and Arkansas men of faith knew a lot more about faith than a New York City boy.

Kenneth Hagin, Kenneth Copeland, and Charles Capps preached over and over on Mark 11:13-14. In fact, the message of "faith" was ringing in my ears as I began to understand why Jesus made sure His disciples understood what He was driving at.

> And seeing at a distance a fig tree in leaf, He went to see if perhaps He would find anything on it; and when He came to it, He found nothing but leaves, for it was not the season for figs. And He answered and said to it, "May no one ever eat fruit from you again!" And His disciples were listening—Mark 11:13-14.

The whole reason Jesus Christ went through this exercise was to teach His disciples about the authority of the believer in regard to the power of the spoken word. To suggest that this is a New Age principle is to accuse Jesus Christ of teaching New Age doctrine! Here we have a biblical example of Jesus Christ speaking to a fig tree and commanding it not to bear fruit.

Notice that verse fourteen says, "His disciples were listening." Obviously, the Lord did this for the express purpose of teaching something to His disciples—that includes us today because we are also His disciples. Later, Jesus made a point of returning to the fig tree. He deliberately went back because He was trying to teach them an important lesson.

> And as they were passing by in the morning, they saw the fig tree withered from the roots up. And being reminded, Peter said to Him, "Rabbi, behold, the fig tree which You cursed has withered"—Mark 11:20-21.

Jesus Christ wasn't strolling around haphazardly cursing fig trees, and the words He spoke were not just some passing or casual remark. He was trying to teach an extremely important principle, which He explained immediately after Peter pointed out the withered fig tree.

> And Jesus answered saying to them, "Have faith in God. Truly I say to you, whoever says to this mountain, 'Be taken up and cast into the sea,' and does not doubt in his heart, but believes that what he says is going to happen, it shall be granted him"—Mark 11:22-23.

Jesus Christ told His followers to have faith in God. Kenneth Hagin teaches that the actual interpretation means "have the God kind of faith." This principle of confessing God's Word, or speaking the Word of faith, comes right out of the Bible, as we have just read. Clearly, it cannot be a New Age teaching.

Remember, the Scriptures are our final authority concerning everything—not the opinions of men. This is how we discern between truth and error. In the final analysis, if you have an argument with this principle that Jesus Christ taught, then you have an argument with the Word of God. We must never compromise the integrity of the Scriptures,

208 *Supernatural Faith In The New Age*

regardless of whether or not they are popular. Christians are to bow their hearts and minds to the Bible in every area of life.

Jesus Christ deliberately and systematically taught His disciples the power and authority they had in the tongue. Just because some people have abused this teaching does not change the truth. Some people mishandle electricity and electrocute themselves, but we don't all stop using electricity.

Moving Mountains

While living in Salt Lake City, I had a tremendous financial need in my business as an independent feature film producer. One evening I was attending a meeting of the Full Gospel Businessmen's Fellowship International, where Richard Shakarian was speaking. He had a word of wisdom that evening for someone who needed a miracle in their business: They could work hard and tunnel through their "mountain" of need; or they could command their "mountain" to move.

After a glorious worship service, we took communion and passed around the bread and grape juice of the Lord's table. Holding hands with my wife Kristina, I felt a supernatural boldness drop into my heart. Then the Holy Spirit revealed that the word to command the mountain to move was for me and my problem.

Next the Lord caused the feature film deal I had been working on for months to come into my mind. The business deal seemed to be stuck with endless meetings in which nothing ever happened. Boldly, I spoke out loud to that mountain of need and commanded every hindrance and obstacle to be removed. In response to a prompting from the Holy Spirit, I made the positive confession that the business plan would come to fruition. The next morning a miracle occurred! A deal that had been hopelessly frozen for months suddenly thawed, and all the hindrances surrounding it melted. Miraculously, a contract involving over a million dollars, as well as a job opportunity, came through.

I have experienced firsthand the powerful teaching in Mark 11:23 and seen God's Word come true. Many times in my life I have spoken to a mountain and dared to confess the answer in the face of adversity and seemingly impossible circumstances.

One time I kept confessing the answer to a situation even though my mind literally reeled from the enormity of the problems facing me. Waves of fear and panic came over me, a horrible sinking feeling grew in the pit of my stomach, and my mind screamed, "You're crazy!" But in the midst of this adversity I confessed the promises of God's Word and spoke the answer to the problem. As I spoke the Word of faith and confessed God's Word, miracles were released. Had I not spoken God's Word and utilized the biblical principle of positive confession, disaster would have occurred.

Confessing God's Word is not a religious game or a superstitious exercise like rubbing a rabbit's foot. It is the practical application of supernatural authority that can prevent disaster and release the Kingdom of God into any situation. By speaking a command in the authority of Jesus Christ, we can take dominion over hellish and negative circumstances.

One night I and a number of friends were in a station wagon that had stalled in the middle of a highway. The ignition had failed, and the lights would not go on. None of us were particularly worried as we tried to start the car because the highway appeared deserted. But all of a sudden, a huge "sixteen wheeler" truck with lights glaring came over the hill and started bearing down on us.

The driver could not see us in the dark. We tried desperately to start the station wagon. From within my spirit I said the word "Jesus." All of a sudden the ignition turned the engine over, the car lights came on, and we sped to safety. The word "Jesus" brought the rescuing miracle power of Almighty God into a situation of almost certain death.

Positive confession of God's Word is not something we can take or leave in the Christian life. Speaking the Word of faith is how we exercise our God-given authority over hell and adverse circumstances. This is an essential, foundational principle in the supernatural Christian life that every child of God must learn to practice if he or she is to walk victoriously and conquer the forces of hell. To strip the believer of this important weapon is like placing an unarmed man in a Roman arena to face a gladiator.

Speaking God's Word is learning how to use the "sword of the spirit" *mercilessly* against the adversary. Not only must we learn to use the power of command and the speaking of God's Word but we must be highly skilled swordsmen who can thrust the devil through with one swift stroke and behead demon powers.

Positive Confession

"Positive confession" is not a *NAM* idea, either. The Bible is a truthful book filled with graphic descriptions of man's failure and the horror of sin. But it is also a very positive book because it teaches that there is a God who loves us and sent a Savior, Jesus Christ, to rescue us and give us hope. In contrast to Jean Paul Sartre's existentialism and the "nothingness" of Eastern mysticism, the reality of a personal God enables us to hold a positive view of reality and think in terms of possibilities.

Western civilization's "high view" of man came into being through the Judeo-Christian world view. As a result, marriage, education, hospitals, democracy, programs for the poor, the judicial system, science, and technology were produced. In contrast, the nation of India is steeped in what could be termed New Age thinking. The result is a "low view" of man that has produced a society with poverty and an oppressive caste system.

Jesus Christ taught us about the authority He has given us and the power of the tongue. The Lord told us that He has given us the "keys of the kingdom" and that we can speak the Word of God in any situation. This biblical principle is the *practical application* of what Jesus Christ taught about the believer's authority.

Unfortunately, many people think they can manipulate the Lord to do their bidding. They have turned positive confession into some kind of magic incantation. But just because some have misused this practice and treated God like some kind of "heavenly Coke machine" does not negate the power or truth of the original biblical principle:

"All things are possible with God"—Luke 18:27.

Finally my brethren whatsoever things are true, whatever is honorable, whatever is right, whatever is pure, whatever is lovely, whatever is of good repute, if there is any excellence and if anything worthy of praise, let your mind dwell on these things—Philippians 4:8.

I have both worked in sales and conducted motivational seminars, and I know how important a "positive mental attitude" is. Maintaining enthusiasm is critical to people who face rejection and obstacles on a daily basis. Many business people and sales professionals who might never attend a church service will attend a sales seminar. In the context of teaching about "motivation" and "selling," it is easy to communicate biblical principles for success and the need for a personal relationship with Jesus Christ.

Popular motivational speakers like Zig Ziglar, who is a leader with the Southern Baptists, and Mary Kay of Mary Kay Cosmetics, have used their "sales" meetings as a "bridge" to share their relationship with Jesus Christ. Thank God for their insight and dedication!

The Power Of Words

In the area of positive confession, there is equal validity in helping people live successful lives through learning to apply the Word of God to any problem or challenge. Many excellent Bible teachers stress the importance of the "positive confession of God's Word." Clearly, confessing God's Word cannot be a *NAM* practice. In his book, *God's Creative Power*, Charles Capps says,

> Words are containers. They carry faith or fear,
> and they produce after their kind. . . . Christianity
> is called the great confession, but most Christians
> who are defeated in life are defeated because they
> believe and confess the wrong things.[1]

Adam and Eve exercised their dominion and authority over the world through the power of the spoken word. Adam was given the privilege of *naming* the animals. In Acts chapter three, Peter *commanded* the lame man: "In the name of Jesus Christ the Nazarene—walk" (verse 6). Even magazines like *Psychology Today* and other scientific journals have published articles on the studies investigating the power of the spoken word in relation to the healing of the physical body.

From the conception of time words have contained power. The Bible is called *God's Word* because it contains power and authority. Man's word also contains power and authority either for good or evil. Adolph Hitler used the evil power of words to seduce and control nations and bring them under the grip of his demonically inspired plan. In today's materialistic culture, biblical teaching on the power of the spoken word is vital if Christians are to realize the full dimensions of their God-given authority through the power of the Word.

Many Christians think that biblical admonishments against "cursing" are to prevent us from speaking four-letter words. If you study the Bible in relation to cursing, however, you will find that it is not simply condemning profanity. It is talking about speaking death to people through the misuse of the spoken word.

Jesus Christ has placed within us the "river of life." We release that river in the lives of other people through the spoken word. We have been given the power to speak "blessing" or "death," and that power is in the tongue. (See Numbers 22:6.)

In his book, *The Secret Kingdom,* Pat Robertson writes,

> We are to take authority by voicing it, whether it involves the devil or any part of the creation. We should not argue with Satan. We merely tell him that he has to go . . . Quite bluntly, we say, "In the name of Jesus, I command you to get out of here, Satan!"
>
> Also, reaching the mind of the Lord, we tell the storm to quiet, the crops to flourish, the

floodwater to recede, the attacking dog to
stop. We simply speak the word aloud.[2]

In 1984, Pat Robertson put these words to work when
he prayed and commanded Hurricane Gloria not to come
near Virginia Beach, Virginia, where his Christian Broadcasting Network studios are located. Miraculously, the storm
did not touch the Virginia coast. Pat Robertson used this
prayer as a test to determine whether or not he should run
for president. According to Robertson, "It was extremely
important, because I felt . . . that if I couldn't move a
hurricane, I could hardly move a nation."[3] As fantastic as
this story sounds, it should be the normal operating proce-
dure for a Christian who understands his authority in Jesus
Christ.

God gave Adam and Eve dominion over this planet, and
we have regained that authority through Jesus Christ. The
only reason we have difficulty comprehending this is
because our culture attempts to lock out the supernatural
through a philosophy of scientific materialism. Furthermore,
we live in a church age that until recently has lost touch
with the power God gave the believer. Miracles, signs, and
wonders were everyday occurrences for the New Testament
church.

Even the most basic reading of the Old and New Testaments reveals the authority and emphasis the Lord places
on words. Confessing and speaking God's Word authorita-
tively and positively is scriptural. Dr. Paul Yonngi Cho, in
his book, *The Fourth Dimension,* says,

> Claim and speak the word of assurance, for your
> word actually goes out and creates. God spoke and
> the whole world came into being. Your word is
> the material which the Holy Spirit uses to create.

So give the word, for this is very important. The church today has lost the art of giving commands. We Christians are becoming perennial beggars, for constantly we are begging. On the bank of the Red Sea Moses begged, "Oh God, help us! The Egyptians are coming." God rebuked him saying, "Moses, why are you crying to me? Give the command and the Red Sea shall be divided."[4]

I was speaking to my sister Caitlin on her birthday, and she asked me if she should confess the promises of God's Word out loud when believing for answers to prayer. My response to her was, "Yes—not as some magic incantation but as a spiritual principle. Conform your mind and tongue to what God says about your life."

Caitlin took these words to heart and has seen many victories in her life. She has become one of the most powerful, loving, and giving Christians I know.

You, too, can be an overcomer by conforming your mind and tongue to God's Word. In other words, never speak fear and unbelief; instead, confess what the Bible says about a situation: "I am more than a conqueror in Christ Jesus" or "perfect love casteth out all fear." (See Romans 8:37 and 1 John 4:18.) This does not mean that you cease being human or become a religious robot who cannot be honest and talk about real feelings. But it does mean that you begin to understand the spiritual power resident in the tongue.

CHAPTER EIGHTEEN
Faith Critics And Robocops

John Lennon sang the words, "I am he as you are he as you are me and we are all together . . . I am the walrus." Clearly, the late Beatle was heavily influenced by Hinduistic philosophy that teaches that we are all one and that each of us is God. This concept is in direct contrast to Scripture, which teaches that there is One God and that each of us is a distinct personality and individual.

There is a growing problem in the evangelical and Christian world: the introduction of existentialist methodology and Eastern mystical thought into Christian theology. The existentialism of Jean-Paul Sartre, Albert Camus, and Karl Jaspers is being wrapped in Christian words by liberal theologians. In addition, the Hinduism and Eastern mystical thought of the *NAM* is working its way into evangelical and Christian circles.

The Final Authority

Although I have defended faith teaching along with certain aspects of positive thinking and the supernatural work of the Holy Spirit in this book, I am *not* embracing everything done *in the name of* faith, positive thinking, and the Holy Spirit. All truth and all revelation must be judged according to some standard.

Christianity is not just one more way to God among many other equally valid ways to God. Jesus Christ is the *only* way to God because He alone is God's Son and the only one who dealt in finality with the sin problem. God has given us a clear method of determining whether or not something is true or not: He has produced the coherent, rational, and verifiable book that we call the Bible.

Martin Luther, the great reformer of the church, said,

> If I profess with the loudest voice and clearest exposition every portion of the truth of God except precisely that little point which the world and the devil are at the moment attacking, I am not confessing Christ, however boldly I may be professing Christ. Where the battle rages, there the loyalty of the soldier is proved and to be steady on the battle front besides, is mere flight and disgrace if he flinches at that point.[1]

There is a grave danger in defining beliefs or theology by an "experience." If the Word of God is not our final authority, then we end up with a belief system built on what secular existentialist philosopher Karl Jaspers termed the "final experience." Our theology becomes based on an inner witness or a subjective experience.

Something cannot be determined to be true merely on the basis of an individual's experience, inner witness, or spiritual revelation. Supernatural manifestations, miracles, signs, or wonders do not in and of themselves prove that something is from God or that it is ultimate truth. People involved in Mormonism, Hinduism, the Unification Church, Eastern mysticism, and the New Age all have had supernatural experiences. Yet, according to the Bible, they are false religions.

In his book, *The New Super Spirituality,* Francis Schaeffer commented on this as it relates to the church:

> With the rise of the new Pentecostalism, we have something different. Often the new Pentecostals put their emphasis on the external signs themselves instead of on content, and they make these external signs the test for fellowship and acceptance. . . .
>
> The rub, of course, is this: there are Unitarian groups and Buddhist groups that have signs. Furthermore, any external sign can be duplicated and counterfeited.[2]

Within the movement toward signs and wonders, the supernatural ministry of Jesus Christ, and dominion theology, certain activities and teachings appear to have strayed from biblical content. We have a responsibility to judge those ideas in light of Scripture, and those who teach such things should be held accountable and challenged. As Dr. Schaeffer points out, experience is not the acid test of whether or not something is from God. There is only one true test, and that is the authority of God's Word.

In another excellent book, *The Great Evangelical Disaster,* Francis Schaeffer wrote,

> . . . the Bible is objective, absolute truth in all areas that it touches upon. And therefore we know that Christ lived, and that Christ was raised from the dead, and all the rest, not because of some subjective inner experience, but because the Bible stands as an objective, absolute authority.[3]

This means that the Bible is true theologically, spiritually, historically, morally, scientifically, and in every area of life. Dr. Schaeffer pointed out that the 1974 Lausanne Covenant read,

> "We affirm the divine inspiration, truthfulness and authority of both Old and New Testament Scriptures in their entirety as the only written Word of God, without error in all that it affirms . . . "[4]

Dr. Schaeffer states that the words "in all that it affirms" are being used as a loophole by some who really mean "but the Bible does not affirm without error that which it teaches in the area of history and cosmos." In other words, some people who signed the Lausanne Covenant do not believe that the Bible is true historically and scientifically.

If the Bible is not reliable historically and scientifically, then it is logical to assume that it contains spiritual error also. Thus, according to this line of reasoning, the Bible may not be absolutely theologically correct. This turns the Bible into a kind of glorified rabbit's foot and leaves the back door open to all kinds of New Age and Eastern mystical beliefs. Dr. Schaeffer concludes by saying,

> Here is the great evangelical disaster—the failure of the evangelical world to stand for truth as truth. There is only one word for this—namely accomodation: the evangelical church has accomodated to the world spirit of the age. First, there has been accomodation on Scripture, so that many who call themselves evangelicals hold a weakened view of the Bible and no longer affirm

the truth of all the Bible teaches—truth not only in religious matters but in the areas of science, history and morality.[5]

When a charismatic says that they have had a "special revelation" concerning the Word of God or that the Holy Spirit has revealed something to them, Christians have the right and *obligation* to judge such teaching in light of Scripture. Such claims must always come under the scrutiny of the Bible to determine their validity. All personal revelation and "inner witness" must be in accordance with scriptural teaching. This is what seperates biblical Christianity from the *NAM* and every other "religious trip."

Dialogue Or Faith-Bashing?

A "Rebuilding the Walls" conference was held recently in Phoenix, Arizona, to examine such subjects as liberation theology, the New Age Movement, Christian mysticism, dominion theology, and inner healing. Writing for *Eternity Magazine*, William Alnor said the "central theme of the conference was that unbiblical and even occultic portions of these doctrines have been accepted by segments of most of the major evangelical denominations and groups in the U.S. today, especially the charismatic, non-denominational churches."[6]

Speakers at the "Rebuilding the Walls" conference included Johanna Michaelsen, author of *The Beautiful Side of Evil*, Dave Hunt, co-author of *The Seduction of Christianity*, Hal Lindsey, author of *Combat Faith*, and Constance Cumbey, author of *Hidden Dangers of the Rainbow*. All of these people have some extremely valid ministries, except Constance Cumbey, who, according to Alnor, implied that

Pat Robertson "might be the antichrist of Revelation." This is so absurd that one might be tempted to laugh were it not so tragic.

Hal Lindsey has influenced millions for Jesus Christ through books like *The Late Great Planet Earth*. He has a tremendous gift for relating the truths of the gospel in an intelligent and relevant manner. In his book *Combat Faith* and on the Trinity Broadcasting Network's "Praise The Lord" program, he has raised some important concerns over "faith teaching."

Despite the fact that "faith bashing" seems to be popular in some quarters of the Christian culture, I don't think it is wrong to have an open dialogue concerning these things. The Body of Christ needs "checks and balances" and accountability based on Scripture. The key thing is to maintain dialogue and disagreements in a spirit of love. Paul Crouch of the TBN Network should be complimented for his courage and fairness in allowing both sides of the "faith debate" on his network. This represents a mature approach often lacking in the Christian culture, which has a tendency to whitewash everything. Hal Lindsey's discussion with Earl Paulk on TBN was refreshing.

Although there have been excesses in the faith movement that needed to be corrected by Scripture, I believe the Christian culture has overlooked a more important issue— the *lack* of faith of large segments of the Body of Christ over the last several centuries. The real problem is not "faith teaching" but the *lack of "faith" in the supernatural power of God* that has given rise to the New Age Movement and a post-Christian culture.

If the church had been doing its job in preaching the gospel of the Kingdom with its emphasis on the gifts of the Holy Spirit, miracles, signs and wonders, faith, love, and the casting out of demons, there would be no

New Age Movement. The *NAM* rushed in to fill the spiritual vacuum created by a liberal Christian church that began to deny the reality of the supernatural in favor of humanistic explanations. One prime area is in the field of counseling.

Without a doubt people need to talk about their problems and their past to qualified Christian counselors and pastors. Talking and listening therapy based on Christian principles probably represents the bulk of Christian counseling. The Holy Spirit is "God's Psychiatrist," and we must use the gifts of the Spirit, such as the word of wisdom, tongues and interpretation, and deliverance. All psychological counseling has a spiritual dimension. Some people are oppressed by spirits of alcoholism, drug addiction, lust, or suicide. Sometimes counselors need to appropriate forgiveness by the power of the Holy Spirit.

Don't Throw The Baby Out With The Bathwater

Although the charismatic movement has been a great blessing to millions of people around the world, there have also been numerous departures from orthodox biblical teaching among its adherents. Teachings such as "discipling" and "shepherding," as well as abuses of faith, positive confession, prosperity, and healing have all come out of the charismatic movement.

Those who proclaim "faith" have sometimes committed serious abuses. One only has to think of Joni Eareckson Tada, a quadriplegic popularized in the Billy Graham film *Joni*. In a recent fund-raising letter, she commented about "the insensitive nature of health-wealth theology" that leaves disabled persons "nearly shipwrecked."[7] Joni has come under criticism and condemnation by some in the faith movement who say she is paralyzed because of her unbelief. If only she would believe God, they say, she would be healed.

Can you imagine Jesus Christ sneering at someone who was terminally ill or quadriplegic and arrogantly telling them to have more "faith"? This is indicative of a lack of spirituality and is the kind of loveless attitude that hinders revival.

After becoming a Christian, I spent a great deal of time reading about and studying faith and positive confession. Soon I was living in the place the apostle Paul wrote about when he said the Kingdom of God is not a matter of talk but of power. (See 1 Corinthians 4:20.)

But although I flowed in the supernatural power of God and experienced numerous miracles, I began to back off from my commitment—not because I thought "faith teaching" was based on *NAM* philosophy but because I saw some excesses on the part of some who claimed to teach "faith." I allowed this to undermine my faith in the supernatural power of God, and the enemy deceived me into adopting a more analytical kind of faith. Developing a subtle posture of superiority and cynicism toward some of those who believed in and practiced the supernatural power of God, I thought I had outgrown the faith movement.

Yes, I still believed in miracles and the blessings of Pentecost, but intellectual pride had sneaked in the back door of my mind. I was no longer enjoying the privileges of exercising my full God-given rights to use the keys of the Kingdom to claim miracles for myself or on behalf of others.

The abuses of faith teaching were and are real, but I made a serious mistake when it came to judging the movement. Not until I attended a "Faith Seminar" given by Dr. Roy Hicks did I understand my error. Dr. Hicks warned, *"Don't throw the baby out with the bathwater"* when it comes to faith.

In other words, just because a few faith teachers are guilty of some abuses and misuses, don't reject the whole thing.

Dr. Hicks was invited to speak at the Church On The Way by Rev. Jack Hayford to give a balanced presentation on faith. One of the primary reasons that Church On The Way continues to grow at such a phenomenal rate is because Rev. Hayford manages to balance teaching on the supernatural power of God with integrity and humility. His church exhibits none of the excesses, showmanship, and manipulation that have characterized a few portions of the charismatic movement that critics term "charismania."

By excesses and showmanship, I do not mean the supernatural manifestations of God, such as miraculous healing, speaking in tongues, the gifts of the Holy Spirit, or praise and worship with uplifted hands. These are not excesses but the normal operating procedures of an authentic New Testament church. What I am talking about is the strutting from the pulpit, the manufactured emotionalism, shoddy fund-raising techniques, and a general lack of integrity that has existed in a small but visible number of charismatic ministries.

The critics of the faith movement have a right to point to these things and say they are not biblical. Critics are wrong, however, when they say that confessing God's Word, the authority of the believer, speaking in tongues, miracles, prosperity, and divine healing are heretical or based on Eastern religions. This is not a criticism of the faith movement but an attack on the very core of the supernatural ministry of the church commissioned by Jesus Christ.

The Author Of Confusion

First Corinthians 14:33 tells us that God in "not the author of confusion." That is the devil's title. Satan uses the criticism and bickering within the Body of Christ to undermine or destroy the power of the believer to heal the sick, set people free, and preach the gospel. His strategy is to weaken believers by undermining faith and thus destroy the effectiveness of the church. The father of lies, therefore, will take a few grains of truth regarding the faith movement and use it to mobilize an all-out assault. The devil would like nothing more than to thwart the Great Commission by stripping the church of its power.

God warns us that "we wrestle not against flesh and blood, but against principalities, against powers, against the rulers of the darkness of this world, against spiritual wickedness in high places" (Ephesians 6:12, *KJV*). An attack on faith is really an attack on the ability of the church and each believer to live victoriously and effectively for Jesus Christ. The devil's principalities and powers attempt to destroy the works of God through the believer. They do this by destroying faith and creating a climate of unbelief, which inhibits the power of God: "And He did not do many miracles there because of their unbelief" (Matthew 13:58).

The way Satan creates unbelief and thus stops the miracles of God is by attacking faith and sowing confusion about the faith teachers. The devil works best in a climate of suspicion, confusion, and paranoia. (See 1 Corinthians 14:33.) One way he accomplishes this goal is to suggest that faith teaching and positive confession is a heresy based on New Age principles.

I am not suggesting that the people making such allegations are willfully or consciously undermining the authority of the church. Many devout, sincere men and women of God have expressed concern over certain faith teachings, and they have some legitimate things to say. We must remember, however, that there is a spiritual dimension to this controversy surrounding faith.

The enemy is exploiting the lack of proper communication and using it to his benefit. This is why it is vital to know what God's Word says—so that you can "quench all the fiery darts of the wicked" (Ephesians 6:16). What are some of the fiery darts? They are the insinuations that the supernatural power of God and faith is of the devil. This creates doubt, unbelief, and confusion.

The recent events in the so-called "Holy Wars" are prime examples of unholy confusion. I am not overlooking the obvious moral failures and financial abuses of a Christian leader. But when the mass media got involved, they salted their bonefide reporting with distortions, misquotes, and ambiguities. In this kind of atmosphere, the kingdom of hell can expand. This is not to blame the media for failures within the church. None of this would have happened if the leader of a large Christian television ministry had been accountable to brothers and sisters in Jesus Christ instead of trying to be a "spiritual Lone Ranger."

Robocops for Jesus

Another way in which the devil can undermine faith is to encourage a kind of mindless and fanatical belief system that encourages people to do foolish things in the name of faith. It is here where the critics of faith teaching have validity to their concerns.

While charismatics have maintained an openness toward the move of the Holy Spirit, they have also demonstrated a susceptability to a kind of super-spirituality. In fact, super-spirituality and pietism have characterized great portions of our contemporary Christian culture, which is unconnected to reality and the world around us.

The leaders of faith teaching have been responsible to teach a balanced and biblical view of faith. A number of groups and people, however, have done some strange things. Faith in the supernatural power of God should not become a weird "snake handling" cult or cause people to do extreme things. The sad fact is that such incidences are happening around the country by people who have seriously distorted faith teaching. The devil would like nothing more than to create a movement of mindless idiots glibly quoting scriptures and championing ignorance and anti-intellectualism.

Jesus Christ is the Lord of all of life not just some pietistic super-spiritual reality. I have encountered a number of people who have become "Ozone Rangers." Through an abuse of faith teaching and an immature understanding of supernatural biblical power, they have entered into a semi-psychotic state where they super-spiritualize everything.

I have met people who in the name of supernatural Christianity seem to have gone on the "Space Mountain" ride in Disneyland permanently. In fact, you cannot carry on a rational, intelligent conversation with them. Every word is a Bible verse, and ordinary life is a kind of cosmic quest. These people have become the "Robocops" of the charismatic movement, clobbering and destroying people in their way.

Sadly, I know of some highly intelligent "fundamentalists" and "evangelicals" who were open to the supernatural power of the Holy Spirit—until a "Robocop for Jesus" arrived and blasted them into disdain. Now they want nothing to do with the power of the Holy Spirit. I wish I could say this was a rare occurrence, but, unfortunately, it is more common than we "charismatics" would like to admit.

The problem starts when an immature person takes certain biblical truths out of context and goes off on a tangent. Jesus Christ wants us to be balanced and intellectual in regard to the supernatural power of the Holy Spirit. Being a fool for Christ doesn't mean we have to leave our minds at home.

God Is Not A Walrus

God loved the world so much that He "sent His only begotten Son" to die for it. (See John 3:16.) As His representatives on earth, we must learn to relate to people without sounding like we're speaking from some ethereal spot in the clouds. The Lord wants us to present the gospel to "all creation" intelligently, practically, and consistently.

Only when people deceived by the New Age Movement and secular humanism understand that the Bible is the absolute standard of truth will they accept the facts: God is *not* a walrus; Satan is the author of confusion; and every person on earth needs a Savior.

CHAPTER NINETEEN

Who's Evangelizing Whom?

The New Age Movement is spreading rapidly through-out our culture and gaining widespread acceptance among the young and upwardly mobile. William Roy, an associate professor of sociology at UCLA, commented on this trend of *NAM* growth in a *Los Angeles Times Magazine* article.

> This is a generation that was raised to be very religious. As we grew up, we became disillusioned with the church, along with everything else. We returned to materialism before we returned to spiritualism.[1]

Nina Easton, who wrote the article in the *Los Angeles Times Magazine* titled "Shirley MacLaine's Mysticism For The Masses" with a subtitle of "She's the Super Saleswoman for the Fast-Growing New Age Movement" commented,

> By no means is this generation ready to give up on materialism, something that shrewd New Age leaders understand. So the movement emphasizes techniques to help its followers deal with the stresses and strains of material life.[2]

The point that these analysts are making is that the *NAM* is growing rapidly because it has rushed in to meet the spiritual needs of a generation that has rejected the church as an answer. Also, the *NAM* communicates a spirituality connected to the real problems of living in a technological and material society. At the same time, evangelicals and charismatics have failed both to penetrate the major power centers of society and to gain mass widespread acceptance among the young.

If this generation was "raised to be very religious" and has tremendous spiritual hunger, then why did it reject the church? When we say this present generation was raised to be religious, we do not mean they were raised to be Christians. This is certainly not the case in a post-Christian culture. What *is* meant is that the spiritually bankrupt philosophy of secular humanism and scientific materialism created a vacuum that left people highly receptive to spiritual things.

Evangelical Jellyfish

The reason the new generation of political leaders, film and television producers, journalists, doctors and nurses, businessmen, artists, writers, teachers, scientists, etc. have often rejected biblical Christianity in favor of New Age mysticism is because Christians have not communicated the same gospel of the kingdom that Jesus Christ preached. Neither have they communicated biblical principles in a relevant and understandable manner.

Too often ministers and preachers spew out theological jargon but don't tell people how Jesus Christ can help solve their daily problems in the areas of money, sex, employment, health, inner healing, and relationships. Christians utter words like redemption, sanctification, eschatology, regeneration, pre-tribulation, and so on, but these terms are meaningless to a post-Christian culture.

In contrast, the *NAM* talks about success, reaching our full potential, prosperity, health, and personal power. While we don't want to turn the gospel of Jesus Christ into a narcissistic and *Me-decade* message, it is important that we learn to communicate to our *present culture* and not to the world of *Father Knows Best* and *Leave It To Beaver.*

Furthermore, a great deal of organized Christian religion is far removed from what Jesus Christ taught and preached. As such, despite all the international conferences on world evangelism, theology, and spirituality, we have reached neither our world nor our nation for Jesus Christ. Twentieth-century Christians have developed a kind of "conference religion" that is not reaching a new generation on a global level. Unfortunately, the New Age Movement is.

Recent Gallup Poll figures tell us that 40 million people in the United States claim to be "born-again" Christians. Simultaneously, we have a moral climate that in many respects is similar to Sodom and Gomorrah. Promiscuity, rampant drug abuse, and the abortion of millions of babies each year seem to negate the Gallup figures. Therefore, Franky Schaeffer's strong words in his book, *Bad News For Modern Man*, do not seem harsh but appropriate:

> Evangelicals are like jellyfish. They float with the tides. They do not direct their own course. Sometimes the currents of the sea beach them. Then they melt in the sun on the sand. Later, they disappear altogether. The jelly dries and no trace is left. The tide goes out, the wind moans softly, and no one notices.
>
> Many Christian leaders, as well as some Christian magazines, periodicals, radio shows, seem

much more interested in finding excuses for not
involving themselves than for actually looking for
ways to involve themselves. The idea of actually
changing the country for better and bringing it into
alignment with Judeo-Christian principles horri-
fies them.[3]

This is a serious problem, and it is imperative that
biblical Christians make the necessary changes to counter-
act the mistakes made. Large portions of the evangelical
and charismatic communities are not open or receptive to
positive change. They are still preaching to the world in
the sociological context of the 1950s.

For example, a quick survey of the geographic power
centers of the evangelical, fundamentalist, and charismatic
spheres of influence will indicate a retreatist position. The
Christian culture is stronger in rural areas such as Texas,
Virginia, and Oklahoma. Southern California, a major
geographic area supposedly with a high percentage of born-
again Christians, has a great influence on the surrounding
culture.

But what Southern California, home of the motion
picture, television, and recording industries, is exporting
around the globe is philosophies and lifestyles. It is the
center of New Age activity, paganism, and hedonism, and
the influence of a pleasure-seeking lifestyle is felt everywhere. New Age magazines like *Whole Life Monthly* are
distributed free at supermarkets, and New Age seminars are
promoted constantly. Meanwhile, one has to hunt to find
any biblical Christian activity. The same is true across the
nation. While the Christian culture has adopted a retreatist
posture, New Age, abortionist, gay-rights, and other radical
groups move aggressively outward.

Spiritual Negligence

Millions upon millions of Americans between the ages of ten and forty have not received the gospel of Jesus Christ in a coherent manner. Major cities like New York, Los Angeles, San Francisco, and Chicago are bursting with people who need to understand the message of God's love for them. Large ghetto populations of Blacks and Hispanics face desperate economic and spiritual conditions. In fact, in many of our major cities the White middle class has been replaced by minorities and single career people. Yet, the majority of evangelistic thrusts are geared toward the rural White middle class. This is reflected in the style of presentation and choice of music by the vast majority of television evangelists.

Not only are the majority of evangelistic and outreach programs targeting a narrow margin of the population, Christians have virtually abandoned the creative arts and multimedia to the secular world. For example, in almost a century of filmmaking, the Christian culture has produced *zero* films that have received critical acclaim and major theatrical distribution. This is a tragic indictment, considering that films and television are the two most powerful means of communication the world has ever known.

Christians are guilty of spiritual negligence! While we drive creative people and intellectuals from the Christian culture with our pietistic attitudes, the *NAM* welcomes artists, filmmakers, and visionaries with open arms. Then we shake our heads and wonder why we have failed to make an impact on society.

Some leaders of the religious establishment are totally removed or insulated from society at large. If this seems like a minor point, let me state quite plainly that this mentality blocks revival. The sad fact is that many Christian leaders and organizations do not return phone calls and ignore letters or proposals; then they turn around and claim to "desire all God has." How can they claim to want all God has for them when they are unreceptive to the Creator speaking through other people?

Translated to its most basic terms, this means that many Christians are not open to new ideas birthed by the Holy Spirit. Someone who is deliberately cut off cannot receive new ideas. This is precisely what happened to the U.S. automobile industry. Executives lost touch with the needs of the American people, and Japanese manufacturers took over. When contemporary Christians ceased preaching the gospel of the Kingdom, the New Age Movement started moving in.

In the same way that U.S. automobile manufacturers realized what was happening and started making changes to recapture the market, so biblical Christians must admit that we have made some serious mistakes and must start making the needed changes. Again, I am not talking about becoming "trendy" but learning how to communicate Jesus Christ's message to this generation. Revival cannot start until there is repentance, and this means a change of mind, attitude, and direction.

Ironically, perhaps the person who best pinpointed this problem is none other than Shirley MacLaine, the "super saleswoman of the New Age":

> The New Age Movement is comprised of mostly successful people. The churches are saying you will find God through poverty . . . Religion wants their allegiance, their power. But successful people don't like to give away their power. . . . So there's a contradiction with

a spiritually expanding person, who is also
successful remaining with the church.[4]

While Shirley Maclaine and other New Age mentors are
getting people excited about their movement, Christians
spend time pointing fingers at anything that moves—
including each other! If anything, the vast majority of
Christian authors writing about the New Age and the occult
spend more time glamorizing the *NAM* than trying to excite
people about the Lord. Many of them have never
experienced the *NAM* firsthand and seemed frightened by
it. Instead of reacting in horror to the movement, we
should be telling people about our great God. Supernatural
Christianity is far more exciting, wondrous, and creative than
anything the New Age has to offer.

Preaching The Full Gospel

Much of the mass culture perceives Christianity as something which negates life. In contrast, they see the New Age
Movement talking about release, creativity, spontaneity, and
human potential. This is a serious problem. Fortunately, a
growing number of gifted, powerful young Christian leaders
have ceased working within the Christian culture in order
to impact society through art, film, television, theatre,
journalism, and other areas where the Christian subculture
discourages participation and creativity. They have not left
Jesus Christ or the church, but they have separated themselves from an arrogant mind-set that alienates the majority
and creates a type of spiritual caste system.

Contemporary Christianity seems almost in opposition
to the gospel of the Kingdom that Jesus Christ preached.
Christians today emphasize a "sin," "failure," and "poverty"
consciousness. It is true that the clear message of the death

238 Supernatural Faith In The New Age

and resurrection of Jesus Christ, salvation, the day of judgment, the holiness of God, and the cleansing of sin through the blood of Jesus Christ must be preached. But we must also preach the *full gospel* , including the Bible's message of healing, prosperity, *and* salvation. Jesus Christ said, "I came that [you] might have life, and might have it abundantly" (John 10:10). The Lord had much to say about total fulfillment and human potential.

Millions of people in the major cities of the world like New York, Los Angeles, Paris, Rome, Moscow, London, etc. have no idea that Jesus Christ died to set them free to be all they were created to be. Then, when the faith teachers preach the gospel with an emphasis on healing, deliverance, and prosperity, they are attacked by critics from many quarters of the Christian culture. Yet, these faith teachers are the ones who have been faithful to preach the same gospel of the Kingdom that Jesus Christ preached!

I am not saying that these men present the gospel perfectly or that there isn't room for growth—especially in the intellectual dimensions of their message. But we must move out of this endless cycle of tearing apart the ministry and message of others and focus on the lost and dying world.

Neither am I negating the importance of loving confrontation with theology that does not conform to the clear teaching of Scripture. As Bible-believing Christians, we must maintain a purity of faith and make sure we do not adulterate the Word of God. Forms of the "world spirit" have entered the church and must be challenged by the Bible. We must not be afraid, however, of emphasizing what God's Word clearly emphasizes.

Dr. Paul Yonggi Cho says in his book, *Salvation, Health & Prosperity*,

. . . people all over the world today are faced
with many problems caused by a sense of nothingness, poverty and curse, and their cries ring out
constantly because of fear of disease and death.
These people need the threefold blessings of Jesus
Christ. During thirty years abroad . . . I saw
clearly that people everywhere were in a situation
which called for a revelation of these blessings.
When this message was preached, many wonderful changes took place and the fire of revival began
to burn.[5]

As God's chosen people living in the world today, it is
our responsibility to take the message of His goodness to
the masses. When we do, hearts will melt and lives will be
changed as the Holy Spirit blazes through the power centers
of our nation. Dare we do less?

CHAPTER TWENTY

Smashing The Gates Of Hell

Our nation and world is in an uproar. Life-threatening crises loom menacingly on the horizon. Political, economic, and social structures are being shaken to their foundations. Modern plagues, including the deadly AIDS, spread daily, pushing medical and scientific resources beyond their limits. Marxist revolution continues to spread in Third World countries, enslaving people under atheistic dictators. Computer-happy bureaucrats erode our basic constitutional freedoms with an invasion of privacy and an increasing dehumanization of individuals.

Western civilization is rapidly approaching a condition that Aldous Huxley wrote about in his book, *Brave New World*. In the book, New Age radicals plot to restructure society into a kind of socialist-Eastern mystical theocracy and usher in a new world order designed to crowd out God.

Today, problems such as pollution, world hunger, and nuclear holocaust seem unsolvable. A recent survey among young people indicated their growing concern over these problems and the question why the church does not seem to do anything about them.

Christian ''Fatalism''

As global pressures increase, many people are beginning to resent Christians who preach the ''end of the world'' without offering any solutions. Intellectuals, politicians, and New Age Movement leaders are alarmed over a conservative Christian political movement that in their eyes seems to delight in the idea of apocalypse—nuclear holocaust as a sign of the end of the age and the rapture of the church.

A kind of "fatalism" has infiltrated many segments of the Christian culture, and the world hears the church saying, "It is too late . . . nothing can be done. The world is going to hell. The antichrist is coming, and we are going to be raptured out of this mess." Is it any wonder that the secular humanistic culture and the New Age Movement see us as a threat to the preservation of civilization?

Christians are seen by many thinking people as the cowboy in the movie *Dr. Strangelove*, directed by Stanley Kubrick. In this "black comedy," a super-conservative cowboy straddles a nuclear missile as he would a horse and, cheering gleefully, rides it as it descends toward its target. The world perceives us as abandoning the earth in a kind of sadistic spiritual mirth, overjoyed that the end is coming and they are going to "get theirs."

We must be honest and admit that this attitude exists in the church and it is wrong! Some Christians even secretly seem to delight in the AIDS epidemic, thinking that God is getting revenge on homosexuals. What kind of warped and loveless Christianity is that? God is not getting revenge on homosexuals. He does not send sickness and disease on people in order to teach them something. When we wrap the wonder of God's grace in petty, sinful, loveless attitudes, no wonder people reject His love. The Lord Jesus Christ died for every member of the human race. God spilled the blood of His Son to rescue every person alive. He loves New Agers, Christians, homosexuals, humanists, atheists—all of mankind.

We must place our petty judgmentalism upon the altar and surrender to God so He can pour His Holy Spirit upon the land. We serve a generous God who will forgive anyone who comes to Him. God does not delight in the destruction of the human race, nuclear holocaust, or AIDS.

Prophecy Fulfilled

Certainly, the Bible speaks of the Second Coming and the rapture as real historical events. The Lord is coming again and soon. The Church of Jesus Christ will be "caught up together" with the Lord, and there will be a new heaven, a new earth, and a day of judgment. (See 1 Thessalonians 4:16-17; Revelation 20:11-15; 21:1.) First, however, many things must take place. The Lord said,

> "For many will come in My name, saying 'I am the Christ,' and will mislead many. And you will be hearing of wars and rumors of wars; see that you are not frightened, for those things must take place, but that is not yet the end. For nation will rise against nation, and kingdom against kingdom, and in various places there will be famines and earthquakes. But all these things are merely the beginning of birth pangs.
>
> "Then they will deliver you up to tribulation, and will kill you, and you will be hated by all nations on account of My name. And at that time many will fall away and deliver up one another and hate one another.
>
> "And many false prophets will arise, and will mislead many. And because lawlessness is increased, most people's love will grow cold. But the one who endures to the end will be saved.

"And this gospel of the kingdom shall be
preached in the whole world for a witness to all
the nations, and then the end shall come"—
Matthew 24:5-14.

Many of these prophecies that Jesus Christ gave regarding His return have already come true. The New Age
Movement, cults, and false religions have produced many
false prophets, gurus, and self-appointed Messiahs. One New
Age group even took out ads in major newspapers around
the world announcing the arrival of "THE CHRIST."

There have been wars, rumors of wars, and earthquakes.
Many who call themselves Christians have fallen away to
serve "strange gods" and have rejected biblical teachings
for Eastern mystical, New Age, and humanistic beliefs.
Lawlessness has increased, and many people's hearts have
grown cold. Divorce, rape, mass murderers, child abuse,
violent crimes, and hideous cases of brutal sadomasochis-
tic killings are evidence of this. Despite all these things, Jesus
Christ said, "And this gospel of the kingdom shall be
preached in the whole world."

The Secret Kingdom

The full-force invasion of the Kingdom of God will
continue around the world while all these terrors are
occurring. The full gospel—salvation, healing, deliverance,
provision, and blessing—will continue to spread. The
message of God's Kingdom is a message of salvation. But
it is also a message on how to bring the infinite power
of God's eternal Kingdom into all areas of life here and
now. In his book, *The Secret Kingdom,* Pat Robertson
says,

From the beginning of man's history, the Lord
has been intent on establishing—through love, not
fear—a kingdom of people who will voluntarily
live under His sovereignty and enjoy His creation.
That is the thrust of His entire revelation made in
what we call the Holy Bible. He is building a kingdom. And a new, major step in that building shows
signs of being at hand. The invisible world may
be ready to emerge into full visibility. One can
almost hear Jesus speaking to His church:
"Beloved, be ready. I have shown you the laws of
my kingdom, the way things truly work. Use
them. Live them. They will work for good even
now."[1]

Jesus Christ is going to return to earth once again! Until
that time comes, however, we have a job to do and people
to rescue. The Christian is not to abandon the people of earth
or convey the idea that we have given up trying to create
positive change. *We are not simply waiting for the rapture.*
As I have stated, Christianity is not fatalism—that is
Hinduism.

Who Will Interpret The Dream?

The book of Genesis tells the story of Joseph supernaturally interpreting the Pharaoh's dream. God gave this young
Hebrew divine answers to the world hunger problem of his
day. In the moment of crisis, God blessed a man with divine
wisdom and gave him a specific plan to save a nation. In
this hour, we need modern Josephs who can interpret
dreams by the power of the Holy Spirit and who have
divine wisdom regarding today's major issues.

Through supernatural revelation, the Holy Spirit wants to provide God's people with solutions to world hunger, nuclear holocaust, and AIDS. We must include world hunger, pollution, peace, and social injustice—along with pro-life, prayer in public schools, and evangelization—in our agenda. This must be accomplished not by conforming to the world spirit or diluting the authority of Scripture but by providing leadership.

We have told an entire generation of Christians that the end is at hand and that the world will get worse and worse until the rapture. Then we wonder why there is a lack of leadership and vision.

Our responsibility to preach the gospel of the Kingdom and bring God's healing force to the major issues of our day is not lessened but *heightened* by the imminence of His return. The prophet Joel said that in the last days God will "pour out" His Spirit "on all mankind." "Young men will see visions"; "Old men will dream dreams"; and believers "will prophesy" (Joel 2:28). *These are the last days*! Right now the Holy Spirit is speaking to the minds and hearts of believers who are open to His work.

The Lord is doing a new thing in the church. He is pouring out the Holy Spirit and giving people all over the world a burning vision. Young people in seminaries, high schools, and universities are being breathed upon by the Holy Spirit as a Third Wave of revival begins to sweep our land.

God desires that *His people* interpret the dream and begin establishing dominion in the name of Jesus Christ. The Lord said, "And I say also unto thee, That thou art Peter, and upon this rock I will build my church; and the gates of hell [or the New Age Movement] shall not prevail against it" (Matthew 16:18, *KJV, italics mine*).

Many Christians assume that this means the church will be able to stand up against the forces of hell. They have developed a "seige mentality," hiding in their churches in fear and watching as the world gets worse and worse. Jesus Christ does not want us to retreat. Empowered by the Holy Spirit, we are to *invade* the powers of darkness.

Spiritual Refugees

The counterculture revolution of the 1960s tried to provide adequate answers or meaningful solutions to the problems of the day. Secular and false prophets rose to interpret the dream and attempted to lead America and the world into a new promised land. Utopian ideas abounded as an entire generation tried to establish a new social order and implement those ideas. When they failed, the winds of change brought apathy, materialism, and quiet despair. In the seventies and eighties, the word *yippie* was replaced by *yuppie*, and the radicals became the establishment.

We live in a time of philosophical bankruptcy and of crisis in leadership. Just as the counterculture of the 1960s was full of hope and ideas, the New Age Movement—the spiritual progeny of the counterculture—is groping for answers. The use of drugs has leveled off, and the radical flamboyance has dwindled somewhat; but underneath it all is the soul of mankind searching for more than survival and materialism.

As a former radical activist, I know what it is like to survey the spiritual barrenness across our land and look desperately for someone to interpret the dreams, to give a vision, and to offer hope. Since I was not presented with true biblical Christianity, I reached out and grabbed the only thing offered to me—the New Age Movement, Eastern mysticism, and socialist revolution.

The refugees of the 1960s are bitterly disillusioned with materialism and the pursuit of pleasure. Along with millions of young people today, they are searching for answers. All of them are groping for someone to interpret the dream for them and lead the way to the promised land. America is beset with a leadership crisis. The scandals rocking the business, political, and religious world are causing people to reel in hopelessness as their leaders fail. It is in this environment that the *NAM* offers false hope and attempts to give people a vision for the future.

But the New Age Movement is a counterfeit to the work of the Holy Spirit, and, like its spiritual predecessor, the counterculture, it is doomed to fall. The *NAM's* plan for a one-world government and a global spiritual order are destined to fail because they are built on the shifting sand of non-truth.

An Army Of Volunteers

History does not stand still. We are rushing toward a confrontation between the forces of hell and heaven. As Satan's counterfeit "pentecost" is poured out upon the earth, the New Age Movement is rising like a great ugly beast trying to engulf and devour mankind. The resurgence of ancient Babylonian practices—astrology, reincarnation, drugs, spiritism, the occult—and seemingly harmless games like "Dungeons and Dragons" and Ouija boards are all designed to deceive and seduce.

Simultaneously, God's true and greater Pentecost—the outpouring of the Holy Spirit—is empowering millions of believers. The words of Ezekiel are coming true:

> The Hand of the Lord was upon me, and He brought me out by the Spirit of the Lord and set

me down in the middle of the valley; and it was full of bones. And He caused me to pass among them round about, and behold, there were very many on the surface of the valley; and lo, they were very dry. And He said to me, "Son of man, can these bones live?" And I answered, "O Lord God, Thou knowest."

Again He said to me, "Prophesy over these bones, and say to them, 'O dry bones, hear the word of the Lord.' "Thus says the Lord God to these bones, 'Behold, I will cause breath to enter you that you may come to life. And I will put sinews on you, make flesh grow back on you, cover you with skin, and put breath in you that you may come alive; and you will know that I am the Lord.' "

So I prophesied as I was commanded; and as I prophesied, there was a noise, and behold, a rattling; and the bones came together, bone to its bone. And I looked, and behold, sinews were on them, and flesh grew, and skin covered them; but there was no breath in them.

Then He said to me, "Prophesy to the breath, prophesy, son of man, and say to the breath, 'Thus says the Lord God, "Come from the four winds, O breath, and breathe on these slain, that they may come to life." ' "

So I prophesied as He commanded me, and the breath came into them, and they came to life, and stood on their feet an exceedingly great army— Ezekiel 37:1-10.

In our generation, the Lord is pouring out the same breath of life that He breathed into the nostrils of man when He formed man out of the dust at Creation: "Then the Lord God formed man of dust from the ground, and breathed into his nostrils the breath of life; and man became a living being" (Genesis 2:7). It is God who has the power to create life—not Satan.

The outpouring of the Holy Spirit in our generation is God breathing life into people so that they can become living people in every dimension of life. The church is beginning to stand on its feet, infused with the breath of life, and becoming "an exceedingly great army."

Targeting The Enemy

It is vital that each believer in Jesus Christ understands his or her place within the context of God's army. This is why I am grieved to hear all the bickering and arguing about faith. Faith and the promises of God are a gift to the church. I am not suggesting there have not been abuses and excesses within what has been called "faith teaching," and I have tried to address some of those issues in this book.

But regardless of where we stand on issues like "faith," we are all soldiers in the great army of the Lord. The purpose of an army is to defend against and defeat any enemy threatening your life or liberty. We have such an enemy, and his name is Satan. He must be the target of all our attacks.

Each of us is responsible to Jesus Christ to give an account of our lives. We all have a strategic place in this space-time spiritual battle. Fundamentalists, evangelicals, and charismatics all have a calling from God and a divine purpose to fulfill. In no way is it my intention to convey an attitude of superiority in calling for a return to a supernatural church.

It is my fervent prayer that as Bible believing Christians we can unite around our Lord and Savior Jesus Christ. I also pray that, despite theological differences, all true Christians who call upon the name of the Lord can move in unity and fulfill the Great Commission. I know of many great saints who do not believe in or practice the gifts of the Holy Spirit yet are faithful to Jesus Christ. Although I believe in the supernatural ministry of Jesus Christ, I recognize the validity of their ministries and callings and have worked with many of these men and women of God.

In the Christian culture, we can have a diversity of opinion without sacrificing unity. There is not necessarily a relationship between the gifts of the Holy Spirit and spiritual maturity. This is why the gifts of the Holy Spirit are often called "grace gifts" (the Greek word is *charis* or *charisma*, from which we get the word *charismatic*). Therefore, I affirm and support the ministries of some of those who have criticized faith teaching and recognize that we are all growing in the grace and knowledge of God.

As the Holy Spirit begins to move upon His people, we will all be convicted in areas in which we have missed the voice of God. Despite our differences, true Christians who affirm the authority of the Scriptures *can* walk arm and arm. We are all part of the family of God and must unite to reach the world for Jesus Christ. "By this all men will know that you are My disciples, if you have love for one another" (John 13:35).

Supernatural Faith

As never before, we must have supernatural faith in the miraculous power of God. This is *not* the time to short-circuit faith in the God of the impossible with excessive theological introspection. Mistakes have been made, but true biblical reformation must occur. We must busy ourselves with the task of reaching this world with the gospel of the Kingdom. Jesus Christ taught us to pray:

> "Our Father who art in heaven, hallowed be Thy name, Thy kingdom come. Thy will be done, on earth as it is in heaven. Give us this day our daily bread. And forgive us our debts, as we also have forgiven our debtors. And do not lead us into temptation but deliver us from evil. [For Thine is the kingdom and the power, and the glory, forever. Amen.]—Matthew 6:9-13.

Jesus Christ wants the earth to be like it is in heaven. In heaven, God's rule and authority prevail. Sickness, disease, poverty, despair, crime, pollution, war, divorce, and crisis are unknown. Our job is to extend God's rule on earth before He returns. All around us people are living lives of quiet desperation. They are waiting for someone to bring them the gospel.

The only hope for mankind is Jesus Christ and the ushering in of His Kingdom. We need a new generation of visionaries and leaders, young and old, who will proclaim the truth to a lost and dying world. Jesus Christ said, "Behold, I say to you, lift up your eyes, and look on the fields, that they are white for harvest" (John 4:35).

Everywhere I go I meet people who are wearied of materialism, hedonism, the New Age Movement, and Eastern mystical religions. They are spiritually hungry and open to the love of Jesus Christ. Now is the time for Christians who have been clothed with power from on high to move forth and reach this world. God is raising up men and women to proclaim the good news of His Kingdom and to transform our society.

The Bible says that the gates of hell *"shall not prevail"* against the church. They cannot withstand the battering ram of the church of Jesus Christ! In other words, the kingdom of hell and the people whom the devil has captured will not be able to oppose the invading force of the Kingdom of God.

But we must be willing to step out in supernatural faith and invade the enemy! God is pouring out the Holy Spirit on believers around the world and infusing them with miracle-working power. The Lord of the universe is impregnating His army with dreams and visions. Will you volunteer? The gates of hell are waiting to be smashed!

> *In this you greatly rejoice, even though now for a little while, if necessary, you have been distressed by various trials, that the proof of your faith, being more precious than gold which is perishable, even though tested by fire, may be found to result in praise and glory and honor at the revelation of Jesus Christ; and though you have not seen Him, you love Him, and though you do not see Him now, but believe in Him, you greatly rejoice with joy inexpressible and full of glory, obtaining as the outcome of your faith the salvation of your souls*—1 Peter:6-9.

APPENDIX

Glossary Of New Age Terms

In defining many of the New Age, Eastern mystical, Buddhist, and Hindu terms, it is important to understand that these words are based on subjective experiences. Although they are actual experiences, they are not "real" in the fullest sense of the word.

In other words, if a person believes that he or she has discovered their "God-consciousness" or has had an experience that leads them to believe they are God, we know from Scripture that they are deceived because there is only one true God. Thus, in the *Glossary of New Age Terms,* the author does not wish to convey the idea by defining these words that they are true in the sense of *absolute truth*. As I discussed in the body of the text, it is vital that the reader learn how to discern between truth and deception by carefully studying the Old and New Testaments.

Altered states of consciousness. A change of the normal waking consciousness or state of mind through the use of psychedelic drugs, meditation, sensory deprivation, ritual, diet, or different modes of thinking.

Arica Institute. A system of spiritual techniques that come from a variety of Eastern mystical practices. This system was developed by Oscar Ichazo and named for his hometown of Arica, Chile.

Astral Projection. The practice of leaving the physical body through soul-travel.

Being one with the universe. The same as God-consciousness, enlightenment, or cosmic consciousness. The concept of self, personhood, and individuality is viewed as an illusion to be transcended.

Cosmic consciousness. An overwhelmingly powerful mystical experience in which a person falsely believes that they have transcended this present reality and merged with a higher consciousness. In reality, this powerful illusion is generated by a cyclically or chemically induced state of consciousness.

Doors of perception. The idea popularized by Aldous Huxley and rock singer Jim Morrison (who named his group the Doors after Huxley's book, *Heaven and Hell and the Doors of Perception*). Followers of the New Age Movement believe that there are doors or paths by which we can leave our present reality and enter the spiritual dimension.

Enlightenment. The Buddhist and Hindu belief in the high state of spiritual being marked by the absence of desire or suffering. Enlightenment is a false spiritual revelation in which a person believes they have found truth. It is not absolute truth as taught by Jesus Christ, however, but a mystical, experiential truth.

EST (Erhard Seminars Training). Named after its founder, Werner Erhard, EST is now called *The Forum.* It is a seminar designed to package Eastern thought in Western terms.

God-Consciousness. The prevalent Eastern mystical and New Age idea that each person is God in their deepest selves. A state of God-consciousness supposedly occurs when a person becomes aware that he or she is God. The purpose of meditation is to produce God-consciousness in an individual. According to the Bible, this is a satanically inspired lie and a demonic delusion.

Karma. The force generated by a person's good or bad actions. Buddhist and Hindu teachings state that if one works on their *karma*, he or she can reincarnate to a higher state of being and reach enlightenment. This is contrary to biblical truth, which teaches that salvation comes as a free gift through faith in Jesus Christ.

LSD (Lysergic Acid Diethylamide). Called by some chemists the most powerful drug known to man, LSD is a psychedelic drug that can cause powerful hallucinatory experiences for ten to twelve hours or more. There are many other drugs with lessor or greater psychedelic properties, such as certain chemically treated strains of marijuana that are capable of producing a strong altered state of consciousness.

Maya. The Eastern mystical belief that this present physical reality is an illusion to be transcended.

Meditation. An Eastern mystical technique for altering the consciousness through the use of a word repeated silently or out loud, such as OM. The purpose of meditation is to quiet the logical or rational mind and awaken the spiritual dimension or God-consciousness within a person.

Nirvana. Paradise or the place a person goes once they have reached enlightenment. Although some New Age proponents teach that when a person achieves enlightenment or *nirvana* their personality remains intact, classic Buddhist teaching reveals that the personality or ego of a person must completely die *before* they become enlightened.

Reincarnation. The concept that when a person dies he or she comes back to this planet. New Agers and mystics believe that through a series of successive lives, a person will finally reach a state of spiritual development in which they are free of the reincarnation cycle—the wheel of endless births and deaths—and achieve enlightenment.

Silva Mind Control. Developed by Jose Silva, this psychological system is designed to let people control their thoughts. *Silva Mind Control* is based in occult and Eastern mystical teaching.

Transcendental Meditation (TM). An ancient system of Hindu meditation developed by Maharishi Mahesh Yogi, who was the spiritual guru to the Beatles. Although *TM* is presented as a science, in reality it is nothing more than ancient Hinduism and the worship of demon gods.

Yin and *Yang.* These terms come from ancient Taoist teachings of the duality that exists in the universe—good and evil, positive and negative, male and female, etc. In this view, the *yin* and *yang* is part of the "great whole."

Notes

CHAPTER ONE

1. Alvin Toffler, *Future Shock* (New York: Random House, 1970), p. 398.

CHAPTER TWO

1. C. S. Lewis, *The Screwtape Letters* (New York: MacMillan, 1970), p. 3.

2. Shirley MacLaine, *Los Angeles Times Magazine,* August 19, 1987, View Section, p. 2.

CHAPTER THREE

1. Richard Alpert, Ph.D., *Remember Be Here Now* (Albuquerque: Lama Foundation, 1971).

2. Shirley MacLaine, *Los Angeles Times Magazine,* August 19, 1987, View Section, p. 2.

CHAPTER FOUR

1. Os Guinness, *The Dust of Death* (Downer's Grove: Inter-Varsity Press, 1973), p. 209.

2. John C. Lilly, *Center of the Cyclone* (New York: Bantam, 1972).

CHAPTER SIX

1. "Financing The Great Commission," *Christianity Today,* May 15, 1987, p. 25.

2. Ibid., p. 39.

3. Ibid.

4. Beth Spring, "Will Pat Run?" *Christianity Today,* August 7, 1987, p. 36.

5. Based on a personal interview with Dr. Fred Price at the Crenshaw Christian Center in Los Angeles, California, November 18, 1987.

CHAPTER SEVEN

1. Dave Hunt and T. A. McMahon, *The Seduction of Christianity* (Eugene, Oregon: Harvest House, 1985), pp. 24-25.

2. Ibid., p. 144.

3. Harold B. Smith, "A Heavy Latter Rain is Expected in Asia," *Christianity Today,* November 7, 1986, p. 50.

4. Dr. Paul Yonggi Cho, *The Fourth Dimension* (Plainfield, New Jersey: Logos, 1979), pp. 100-101.

5. Kenneth Hagin, *New Thresholds of Faith* (Tulsa: Faith Library Publications, 1986), p. 42.

6. Kenneth Copeland, *The Laws of Prosperity* (Greensburg, Pennsylvania: Manna Christian Outreach, 1974), p. 14.

CHAPTER NINE

1. Tim Stafford, "Testing the Wine From John Wimber's Vineyard," *Christianity Today,* August 8, 1986, p. 18.

2. Ibid.

CHAPTER TEN

1. Charles Finney, *Power From On High* (Washington, Pennsylvania: Christian Literature Crusade, 1979), p. 11.

2. Ibid., p. 9.

3. Ibid., p. 24.

4. Francis Schaeffer, *The Great Evangelical Disaster* (Westchester, Illinois: Crossway, 1984), p. 141.

CHAPTER ELEVEN

1. Bruce Barron, "Faith Healers: Moving Toward The Mainstream," *Christianity Today,* July 10, 1987, p. 50.

2. Ibid.

3. Ibid.

4. Hunt and McMahon, *The Seduction of Christianity,* p. 219.

CHAPTER TWELVE

1. Franky Schaeffer, *Addicted to Mediocrity* (Westchester, Illinois: Crossway, 1981), pp. 27-28.

2. Jack W. Hayford, *Above and Beyond* (Van Nuys, California: Living Way Ministries, 1986), p. 23.

CHAPTER THIRTEEN

1. Cho, *The Fourth Dimension,* p. 44.

2. Dr. Roy Hicks, *Keys of the Kingdom* (Tulsa: Harrison House, 1984), pp. 8-9.

3. Ibid., pp. 10-11.

4. Cho, *The Fourth Dimension,* p. 44.

CHAPTER FOURTEEN

1. Hagin, *New Thresholds of Faith,* p. 54.

2. Ibid., p. 55.

3. Ibid.

4. Ibid., p. 56.

5. John W. Tranter, Jr., *Images* (Springdale, Pennsylvania: Whitaker House, 1986), p. 23.

CHAPTER FIFTEEN

1. *Charisma,* June, 1987, p. 65.

2. Charles Colson, "My Cancer and the Good Health Gospel," *Christianity Today,* April 3, 1987, p. 56.

3. Kenneth Hagin, Jr., *Ministering to the Brokenhearted* (Tulsa: Faith Library Publications, 1987), p. 7.

4. Ibid., p. 21.

5. "Fuller Seminary Releases Study on the Miraculous," *Christianity Today,* February 6, 1987, p. 44.

6. Ibid., p. 45.

7. Bruce Barron, "Faith Healers: Moving Toward the Mainstream," *Christianity Today,* July 10, 1987, p. 50.

CHAPTER SIXTEEN

1. *Fortune,* August 31, 1987, p. 93.

2. Pat Robertson with Bob Slosser, *The Secret Kingdom* (Nashville: Thomas Nelson, 1982), p. 69.

3. Hagin, *New Thresholds of Faith,* p. 13.

4. Dr. Fred Price, Sunday Worship Service Tape, Crenshaw Christian Center, Los Angeles, California.

CHAPTER SEVENTEEN

1. Charles Capps, *God's Creative Power* (Tulsa: Harrison House, 1976), p. 4, 1.

2. Robertson, *The Secret Kingdom,* p. 209.

3. Beth Spring, "One Step Closer to the Oval Office," *Christianity Today,* October 17, 1986, p. 45.

4. Cho, *The Fourth Dimension,* pp. 31-32.

CHAPTER EIGHTEEN

1. Schaeffer, *The Great Evangelical Disaster,* p. 50.

2. Francis Schaeffer, *The New Super-Spirituality* in "The Complete Works of Francis Schaeffer" (Westchester Illinois: Crossway, 1972), p. 391.

3. Schaeffer, *The Great Evangelical Disaster,* p. 55.

4. Ibid., p. 56.

5. Ibid., p. 37.

6. "Rebuilding Conference on Bad Theology," *Eternity Magazine,* June 1987, p. 35.

7. Bruce Barron, "Faith Healers: Moving Toward the Mainstream," *Christianity Today,* July 10, 1987, p. 50.

CHAPTER NINETEEN

1. Nina Easton, "Shirley MacLaine's Mysticism For The Masses," *Los Angeles Times Magazine,* September 6, 1987, p. 9.

2. Ibid.

3. Franky Schaeffer, *Bad News For Modern Man* (Westchester, Illinois: Crossway, 1984), p. 45.

4. Easton, *Los Angeles Times Magazine,* p. 32.

5. Dr. Paul Yonggi Cho, *Salvation, Health, and Prosperity* (Altamonte Springs, Florida: Creation House, 1987), p. 12.

CHAPTER TWENTY

1. Robertson, *The Secret Kingdom,* p. 212.

Recommended Reading

Capps, Charles. *God's Creative Power* (Tulsa: Harrison House, 1976).

Cho, Dr. Paul Yonggi. *The Fourth Dimension* (Plainfield, New Jersey: Logos, 1979).

Cho, Dr. Paul Yonggi. *Salvation, Health, and Prosperity* (Altamonte Springs, Florida, 1987).

Copeland, Kenneth. *The Laws of Prosperity* (Greensburg, Pennsylvania: Manna Christian Outreach, 1974).

Finney, Charles G. *Crystal Christianity* (Springdale, Pennsylvania: Whitaker House, 1985).

Finney, Charles G. *Power From on High* (Washington, Pennsylvania, 1979).

Guinness, Os. *The Dust of Death* (Downer's Grove, Illinois: InterVarsity Press, 1973).

Hagin, Kenneth. *New Thresholds of Faith* (Tulsa: Faith Library Publications, 1986).

Hagin, Kenneth, Jr. *Ministering to the Brokenhearted* (Tulsa: Faith Library Publications, 1987).

Hayford, Jack W. *Above and Beyond* (Van Nuys, California: Living Way Ministries, 1986).

Hicks, Roy. *Keys of the Kingdom* (Tulsa: Harrison House, 1984).

Lewis, C. S. *The Screwtape Letters* (New York: MacMillan, 1970).

Robertson, Pat and Slosser, Bob. *The Secret Kingdom* (Nashville: Thomas Nelson, 1982).

Schaeffer, Francis. *A Christian Manifesto* (Westchester, Illinois: Crossway, 1981).

Schaeffer, Francis. *The Great Evangelical Disaster* (Westchester, Illinois: Crossway, 1984).

Schaeffer, Francis. *How Should We Then Live?* (Westchester, Illinois: Crossway, 1976).

Schaeffer, Francis. *The New Super-Spirituality* (Westchester, Illinois: Crossway, 1972).

Schaeffer, Franky. *A Time for Anger: The Myth of Neutrality* (Westchester, Illinois: Crossway, 1982).

Schaeffer, Franky. *Addicted to Mediocrity* (Westchester, Illinois: Crossway, 1981).

Schaeffer, Franky. *Bad News For Modern Man* (Westchester, Illinois: Crossway, 1984).

Tranter, John W., Jr. *Images (Springdale, Pennsylvania: Whitaker House, 1986).*

About The Author

Paul McGuire is an independent producer of feature films that have been seen in theaters around the world. He was the executive producer of the PG-rated comedy, *Knocking at Heaven's Door,* and of a science fiction film that was a best-seller at the Cannes film festival in France. Paul was the executive producer-executive vice president of Franky Schaeffer's Hollywood-based feature film company, Schaeffer Buchfuehrer Productions. He has been interviewed by the *New York Times, Daily Variety, The Hollywood Reporter, Screen International, Cinefantastique, ABC-TV,* the *Associated Press,* and *United Press International.*

Growing up in New York City, Paul demonstrated with radical activist Abbie Hoffman and was made an honorary member of the Black Panther Party. He studied altered states of consciousness, along with film and psychology, at the University of Missouri. After being a practicing mystic for many years, Paul became deeply involved with meditation, parapsychology, and the occult.

Then Paul McGuire experienced the true meaning of "revolution and liberation" when he had an overwhelming encounter with the Person of Jesus Christ. He was born again and for the first time in his life discovered what freedom was all about.

Paul has been active with *Campus Crusade For Christ* and *The Full Gospel Businessmen's Fellowship International*. He and his wife, actress Kristina McGuire, attend the Church On the Way in Van Nuys, California.

For information regarding speaking engagements, or to purchase the video tape, *Supernatural Faith in the New Age*, write

Paul McGuire
P. O. Box 713
Hollywood, California 90078